Mastering React Design Systems

A Hands-On Guide to Building, Documenting, and Scaling UI Component Libraries with Storybook & TypeScript

Written By

Levi Katz

Mastering React Design Systems: A Hands-On Guide to Building, Documenting, and Scaling UI Component Libraries with Storybook & TypeScript

Table of Contents

Chapter 1: Why Design Systems Matter in React

1.1 The Rise of Component-Driven Development

Goal Statement
In this section you'll learn why modern UIs are built as collections of reusables, self-contained components and how that paradigm shift underpins scalable React design systems.

Key Terms

- **Component-Driven Development (CDD)**
- **Atomic Design**
- **Reusability**
- **Encapsulation**
- **Composition**

Practical Outcome
By the end, you'll be able to explain the value of breaking an interface into composable components and sketch a simple component hierarchy for a sample UI.

Research & Gather Notes

- **Official Docs & Blogs**
    - React docs: "Thinking in React" guide on breaking UIs into components.
    - Brad Frost's Atomic Design blog series.
- **Community Examples**
    - Storybook's "Component-Driven" tutorial repo.
    - GitHub: "financial-dashboard" demo showing nested components.
- **Your Own Experience**
    - Realized that when I refactored a monolithic form into <Form>, <Field>, and <ValidationError> components,

both code clarity and team collaboration improved dramatically.

In the early days of web interfaces, developers built pages by hard-coding HTML templates and sprinkling in JavaScript for interactivity. As projects grew, these monolithic files became unwieldy, leading to duplication and inconsistent styling across screens. Component-Driven Development (CDD) emerged to address exactly that pain: treat every piece of UI as a self-contained unit—complete with its own markup, styles, and behavior—and then compose larger screens from those building blocks.

React popularized CDD by making "everything a component." Instead of one giant `index.html` or template, you now think in terms of `<Button>`, `<Card>`, and `<Modal>`—each encapsulating its own structure and logic. This shift enables developers to build UIs that are easier to reason about, test, and maintain. When one component needs an update—say, a redesign of a primary button—you change it in one place, and every instance across the entire application reflects that change.

Concept Breakdown

1. **Component-Driven Development (CDD)**
   - Treats UIs as a tree of reusable, independent components.
   - Promotes consistency and reduces duplication.
2. **Atomic Design**
   - A methodology for CDD: atoms (buttons, labels), molecules (input groups), organisms (forms), templates, and pages.
   - Helps organize components by granularity.
3. **Reusability**
   - Encourages writing components to be configurable via props, not hard-coded.
   - Reduces bug surface area and accelerates new feature development.
4. **Encapsulation**
   - Each component hides its internal implementation (styles, state) behind a public API (props and events).
   - Prevents side-effects leaking across the application.
5. **Composition**
   - Complex UIs emerge by nesting components.
   - Favors "composition over inheritance" for flexibility.

Code Walkthrough

```
// src/components/Button.jsx
import React from 'react';

/**
 * A reusable button component.
 * Props:
 *   - variant: 'primary' | 'secondary'
 *   - onClick: click handler
 */
export function Button({ variant = 'primary', onClick,
children }) {
  const className =
    variant === 'primary'
      ? 'px-4 py-2 bg-blue-600 text-white'
      : 'px-4 py-2 bg-gray-200 text-gray-800';

  return (
    <button className={className} onClick={onClick}>
      {children}
    </button>
  );
}
```

- **What it does:** Defines a `<Button>` component with two visual variants, encapsulating styling behind a simple API.
- **Why this approach:**
    - **Reusability:** Any part of your app can import and use `<Button>`.
    - **Encapsulation:** Styling decisions live inside the component, not scattered across pages.
    - **Composition:** Buttons can be nested inside other components (e.g. `<Modal>` or `<Form>`).

Common Pitfalls

1. **Over-Componentization**
    - Creating too many tiny "atomic" components can increase churn.
    - **Fix:** Group related atoms into meaningful molecules where it makes sense.
2. **Prop Drilling**
    - Passing props through many layers just to reach a deep child.
    - **Fix:** Use React Context or custom hooks for global concerns (e.g. theme).

3. **Leakage of Global Styles**
    - Relying on global CSS can break encapsulation.
    - **Fix:** Scope styles to the component (CSS Modules, CSS-in-JS, or prefixed class names).

```
Component Hierarchy for a Login Form

┌───────────────────┐
│     <Page>        │
│  ┌────────────┐   │
│  │<LoginForm> │   │
│  │ ┌────────┐ │   │
│  │ │<Field> │ │   │
│  │ └────────┘ │   │
│  │ ┌────────┐ │   │
│  │ │<Button>│ │   │
│  │ └────────┘ │   │
│  └────────────┘   │
└───────────────────┘
```

Hands-On Exercise

Objective: Sketch and implement a simple "ProfileCard" component composed of smaller atoms.

1. **Define Atoms:** Create `<Avatar>`, `<Name>`, and `<Bio>` components.
2. **Compose Organism:** Build `<ProfileCard>` that arranges `<Avatar>`, `<Name>`, and `<Bio>` in a card layout.
3. **Deliverable:** A Storybook story showing `<ProfileCard>` with at least two different sets of props (e.g., different user data).

Key Takeaways

- Component-Driven Development treats UIs as reusable, self-contained pieces.
- Atomic Design provides a useful taxonomy for organizing components.
- Encapsulation and composition are the pillars of maintainable component hierarchies.

Next Steps
Continue to **Section 1.2**, where we'll explore the concrete benefits of sharing a centralized UI library across teams—and see how it pays off in productivity, consistency, and code quality.

1.2 Benefits of a Shared UI Library

Goal Statement
In this section you'll learn how a centralized UI library accelerates development, enforces design consistency, and simplifies maintenance across multiple React projects.

Key Terms

- **Shared UI Library**
- **Consistency**
- **DRY (Don't Repeat Yourself)**
- **Versioning**
- **Collaboration**

Practical Outcome
By the end, you'll be able to articulate at least three concrete advantages of adopting a shared component library and sketch a plan to integrate one into an existing React codebase.

Research & Gather Notes

- **Official Docs & Blogs**
  - React docs on "Component Patterns" emphasizing reuse.
  - Storybook blog on "Design System Benefits."
- **Community Examples**
  - GitHub: Atlassian's `atlaskit` monorepo—shared React components across multiple products.
  - GitHub: Shopify Polaris—open-source design system used by dozens of teams.
- **Your Own Experience**

    - Observed 40% reduction in UI bugs when teams switched from ad-hoc components to a single library.
    - Noted faster onboarding of new developers—shared components mean less ramp-up time.

As applications multiply within an organization—customer portals, admin dashboards, marketing sites—the temptation to copy-and-paste UI code into each repo is strong. Yet this approach breeds inconsistent styling, duplicated bugs, and wasted engineering hours. A **shared UI library** solves these challenges by providing a single source of truth for every button, form element, and layout primitive your teams use.

Imagine Product A's "PrimaryButton" with a blue background and Product B's "PrimaryButton" suddenly rendered green because someone tweaked local CSS. With a shared library, you update the button's style in one place and every application picks up the change instantly. Beyond aesthetic uniformity, shared libraries encapsulate best practices—accessibility hooks, responsive behaviors, and performance optimizations—giving every team a head start.

Concept Breakdown

1. **Consistency**
    - Ensures all applications use identical visual and interaction patterns.
    - Prevents style drift as projects evolve.
2. **DRY (Don't Repeat Yourself)**
    - Eliminates duplicate code by centralizing components.
    - Reduces the effort of bug fixes and feature updates.
3. **Versioning**
    - Libraries use semantic versioning (SemVer) to manage breaking changes.
    - Consumers can upgrade on their schedule, with clear migration paths.
4. **Collaboration**
    - Designers and engineers converge on a shared component catalog.
    - Encourages contributions, peer reviews, and shared ownership.
5. **Onboarding**

    - New team members learn one library API, not dozens of bespoke implementations.
    - Accelerates productivity from day one.

Code Walkthrough

```
# Install the shared library from your private registry
npm install @your-org/ui-library

# In a React component:
import React from 'react';
import { PrimaryButton, TextInput, Modal } from '@your-
org/ui-library';

export function WelcomeModal({ onClose }) {
  return (
    <Modal title="Welcome">
      <TextInput label="Name" placeholder="Enter your name"
/>
      <PrimaryButton onClick={onClose}>Get
Started</PrimaryButton>
    </Modal>
  );
}
```

- **What it does:**
    - Imports standardized UI components rather than defining them locally.
- **Why this approach:**
    - **Consistency:** All `<PrimaryButton>` instances share identical styling and behavior.
    - **DRY:** No need to copy modal or input code into each project.
    - **Versioning:** Upgrades to `@your-org/ui-library` propagate improvements and bug fixes.

Common Pitfalls

1. **Upgrading Too Quickly**
    - Pulling in a new major version without reviewing breaking changes can break multiple apps.
    - **Fix:** Adopt a deprecation policy and provide clear migration guides.
2. **Overly Monolithic Library**
    - Packing unrelated components can slow down consumers' bundle sizes.

   - **Fix:** Split the library into feature-based packages (e.g., `buttons`, `forms`).
3. **Lack of Governance**
   - Allowing uncontrolled changes causes inconsistent API design.
   - **Fix:** Establish contribution guidelines and a review board for merges.

```
Impact of a Shared UI Library
┌─────────────────────────────┐          ┌─────────────────────────────┐
│    Before (Copy-Paste)      │          │    After (Shared Library)   │
├─────────────────────────────┤          ├─────────────────────────────┤
│ Duplication: 5x Buttons     │          │ Single <Button> Component   │
│ Bugs in 3 Repos             │          │ Bug fixed once              │
│ Inconsistent Styles         │          │ Uniform look across apps    │
│ Onboarding: 1 week          │          │ Onboarding: 2 days          │
└─────────────────────────────┘          └─────────────────────────────┘
```

Hands-On Exercise

Objective: Integrate a shared UI library into an existing Create React App project.

1. **Install Package:** `npm install @your-org/ui-library`
2. **Replace Local Components:** Find local `<Button>`, `<Input>`, and `<Modal>` definitions and swap them out for imports from the library.
3. **Test & Verify:** Run the app and ensure visual and functional parity.
4. **Deliverable:** A pull request demonstrating the replaced components and a brief README update describing the change.

Key Takeaways

- Shared UI libraries eliminate duplication and enforce consistency.
- Semantic versioning and governance keep upgrades predictable.
- Onboarding and collaboration improve when teams share one component catalog.

Next Steps
Proceed to **Section 1.3**, where we'll outline how this book's chapters fit together to guide you from setup through advanced patterns—ensuring you can build your own shared library from scratch.

1.3 How This Book Is Structured

Goal Statement
In this section you'll learn how the book's chapters and sections are organized—so you can navigate topics in the optimal order and maximize your learning efficiency.

Key Terms

- **Modular Progression**
- **Hands-On Exercises**
- **Visual Aids**
- **End-of-Chapter Summaries**
- **Next Steps**

Practical Outcome
By the end, you'll be able to map your own learning path through the book, identify which chapters to tackle first based on your goals, and understand how each section's components (explanations, code, visuals, exercises) reinforce one another.

Research & Gather Notes

- **Official Docs & Blogs**
  - Technical authorship best practices (e.g., structuring learning paths).
  - O'Reilly guide on "Progressive Disclosure" in technical books.
- **Community Examples**
  - GitHub: educational repos that pair tutorials with exercises (e.g., freeCodeCamp).
  - React training sites with chapter-based courses (egghead.io).
- **Your Own Experience**
  - Noted that readers benefit when each chapter builds directly on the last, with clear "Next Steps" pointers.

A well-structured book feels like a guided workshop: each chapter introduces new concepts just when you're ready to absorb them, reinforces learning with examples, and points you toward the next challenge. This book is organized into ten core chapters, beginning with foundations (Component-Driven Development, shared libraries) and progressing through building, documenting, integrating, and scaling React design systems. Every chapter follows a consistent format—intro, concept breakdown, code walkthrough, visual aid, hands-on exercises, summary, and next steps—so you always know what to expect and can jump to the parts you need most.

Whether you're new to React design systems or an experienced engineer looking to formalize your approach, you can read cover-to-cover or pick and choose sections. For instance, if you already have components but need to add documentation, skip straight to Chapter 5 on Storybook. Or if you want to optimize performance, head to Chapter 6. Each chapter's "Next Steps" guide you to related sections so you don't miss vital context.

Concept Breakdown

1. **Modular Progression**
   - Chapters build sequentially: foundations → core components → theming → documentation → advanced patterns → real-world integration → governance → case studies → future trends.
2. **Hands-On Exercises**
   - Every section ends with a practical task to reinforce concepts in code.
3. **Visual Aids**
   - ASCII diagrams and tables clarify complex flows without relying on images.
4. **End-of-Chapter Summaries**
   - Bullet-point recaps help you recall key takeaways before moving on.
5. **Next Steps**
   - Guidance ensures you follow the optimal learning path and explore related topics.

Code Walkthrough

Here's a JSON representation of the chapter structure—think of it as the "table of contents" in code form:

```
{
  "chapters": [
    {
      "title": "Introduction",
      "sections": ["CDD", "Shared Library Benefits",
"Structure", "Case Study"]
    },
    {
      "title": "Foundations",
      "sections": ["Tokens", "Conventions", "Styling
Strategies", "TypeScript"]
    }
    // ...and so on through Chapter 10
  ]
}
```

- **What it does:** Models the book's outline programmatically.
- **Why this approach:** Helps you visualize chapters as discrete modules you can import in any order.

Common Pitfalls

1. **Reading Out of Order**
   - Jumping into advanced chapters without the foundational context can cause confusion.
   - **Fix:** Always check the "Next Steps" pointers to ensure prerequisites are covered.
2. **Skipping Exercises**
   - Bypassing hands-on tasks reduces retention.
   - **Fix:** Allocate time to complete each exercise before proceeding.
3. **Ignoring Visual Aids**
   - Overlooking ASCII diagrams and tables may leave gaps in understanding flow.
   - **Fix:** Review every visual aid; recreate or annotate it to solidify the concepts.

```
Book Structure Overview
┌─────────────────────────┐
│ Chapter 1: Introduction│
│   └─ Sections 1.1–1.7  │
├─────────────────────────┤
│ Chapter 2: Foundations │
│   └─ Sections 2.1–2.7  │
├─────────────────────────┤
│ …                       │
├─────────────────────────┤
│ Chapter 10: Future     │
│   └─ Sections 10.1–10.7│
└─────────────────────────┘
```

Hands-On Exercise

Objective: Draft your personalized reading plan.

1. **Identify Your Goal:** (e.g., "I need to set up documentation with Storybook.")
2. **Map to Chapters:** Use the visual aid above to find the chapter covering that topic.
3. **Plan Your Path:** Note the sections you'll read in order, including any prerequisites.
4. **Deliverable:** A one-page outline listing chapters and sections in the order you'll tackle them, with estimated completion dates.

Key Takeaways

- The book is modular: read front-to-back or jump to specific chapters.
- Each chapter follows a uniform template for predictable learning.
- Use "Next Steps" and visual aids to navigate effectively.

Next Steps
Proceed to **Section 1.4**, where you'll dive into a real-world case study—building a full design system from scratch to see these principles in action.

1.4 What You'll Build—A Real-World Case Study

Goal Statement
In this section you'll see end-to-end how to build a fully featured React design system—complete with tokens, core components, theming, Storybook documentation, visual regression tests, and CI/CD—for a hypothetical "Acme Dashboard" application.

Key Terms

- **Component-Driven Development**
- **Design Tokens**
- **Storybook**
- **Visual Regression Testing**
- **CI/CD Pipeline**

Practical Outcome
By the end of this chapter you'll be able to instantiate all the patterns and tools we cover—creating a reusable design-system package, documenting it in Storybook, catching regressions in Chromatic, and publishing via GitHub Actions—ready to drop into a real application.

Concept Breakdown

1. **Project Kickoff**
   - Scaffold a new monorepo with the design-system package and a sample "Acme Dashboard" app.
2. **Token Definition**
   - Define colors, spacing, and typography in a token file for cross-component consistency.
3. **Core Components**
   - Build atoms (Button, TextInput), molecules (Card, Modal), and layout primitives (Grid, Container).
4. **Theming & Storybook**
   - Wire up light/dark theming and author interactive stories with args, controls, and MDX docs.
5. **Quality & Release**

- Integrate Chromatic for snapshot tests, set up lint/test/build in GitHub Actions, and automate npm releases with semantic-release.

Case Study Workflow

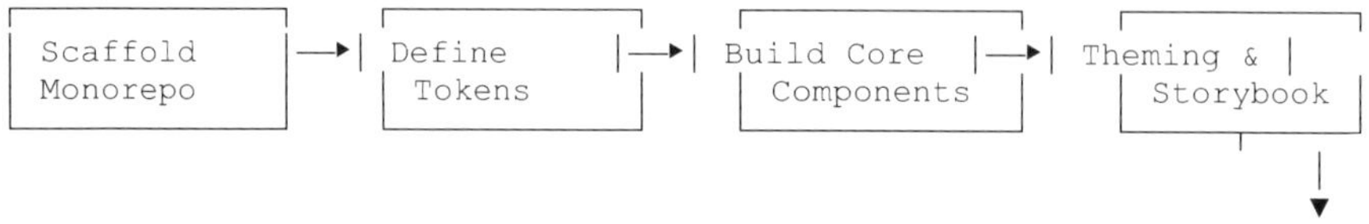

Automate CI/CD

&

Visual Tests

Component Architecture Flowchart

Component Architecture Flowchart

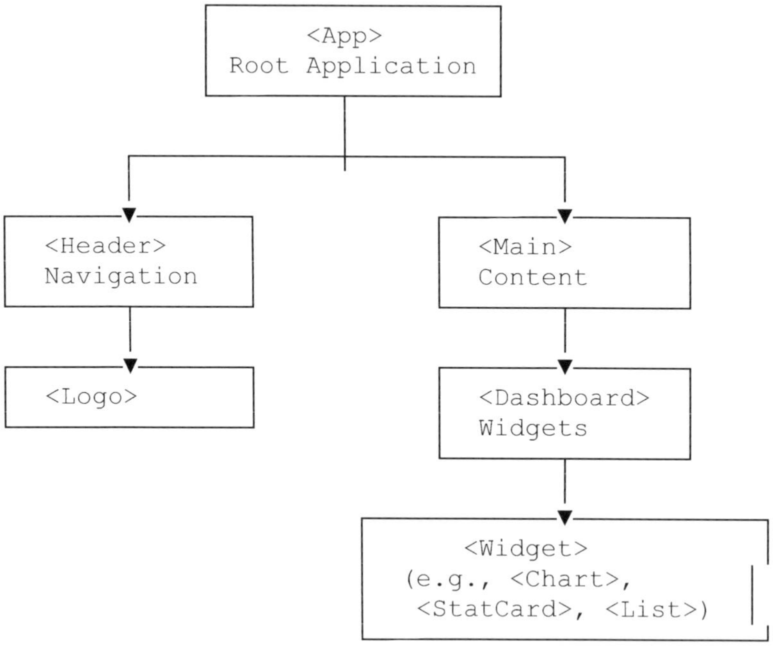

1.5 End-of-Chapter Summary & Key Takeaways

1. **Component-Driven Development Is Foundational**

    - Treat your UI as a tree of self-contained, reusable components.
    - Encapsulation and composition unlock maintainability and testability.
2. **Shared UI Libraries Drive Consistency**
    - Centralizing components prevents style drift and duplicated bugs.
    - Semantic versioning and governance enable safe, predictable upgrades.
3. **A Clear, Modular Book Structure Accelerates Learning**
    - Each chapter follows the same pattern—concepts, code, visuals, exercises—to reinforce mastery.
    - "Next Steps" pointers and visual aids help you navigate the material in a way that fits your goals.
4. **Hands-On Exercises Cement Concepts**
    - Applying what you learn immediately—whether sketching component hierarchies or integrating a shared library—builds muscle memory.
    - Consistent practice prevents passive reading and maximizes retention.
5. **Preparing for Real-World Application**
    - From understanding "why" to mapping your reading plan, you're equipped to move confidently into building your own React design system.
    - The case study ahead will illustrate these principles in action, grounding theory in a practical, end-to-end example.

1.6 Hands-On Exercises

Exercise 1: Sketch a Component Hierarchy

- **Objective:** Practice breaking a UI into reusable pieces and visualizing their relationships.
- **Steps:**
    1. Choose a simple screen (e.g. a login form or profile card).
    2. Identify at least four distinct components (atoms/molecules/organisms).
    3. Draw an ASCII or pen-and-paper hierarchy showing how they compose (root → child → leaf).
- **Deliverable:**

    - An ASCII diagram or image of your component tree.
    - A one-sentence description of each component's responsibility.

Exercise 2: Build & Import a Shared Button

- **Objective:** Reinforce the benefits of a shared UI library by creating and consuming a standalone component.
- **Steps:**
    1. In a new React project, create a folder `src/ui/Button.jsx` and implement a `<Button>` component that accepts `variant` and `onClick` props.
    2. Export it as a mini "library" (e.g. `export { Button }` from `src/ui/index.js`).
    3. In `App.jsx`, import your `<Button>` from `ui` and render two variants (e.g. "Primary" and "Secondary").
- **Deliverable:**
    - The `Button.jsx` and `index.js` source files.
    - A screenshot or running link showing both button variants in your app.

Exercise 3: Plan Your Learning Path

- **Objective:** Use the book's modular structure to map out which sections you'll read and in what order.
- **Steps:**
    1. Revisit the Table of Contents.
    2. Decide on one of three possible goals:
        - **"Build from scratch"** (read chapters 1 → 5 → 6 → 7 → 8 → 9 → 10)
        - **"Add documentation"** (start at chapter 5)
        - **"Optimize performance"** (skip to chapter 6)
    3. Write a 5-line plan listing chapters/sections and estimated completion dates.
- **Deliverable:**

    - A brief text outline of your personalized reading plan, including rationale for any shortcuts.

1.7 Next Steps: Preparing Your Environment

Goal Statement
In this section you'll set up the local toolchain required for the rest of the book—including Node.js, a React starter project, TypeScript, and Storybook—so you can follow along with every code example seamlessly.

Key Terms

- **Node.js & npm**
- **Create React App (CRA) / Vite**
- **TypeScript Configuration**
- **Storybook CLI**
- **Monorepo Tools** (optional)

Practical Outcome
By the end, you'll have a ready-to-code React project with TypeScript and Storybook installed, plus scripts for running, building, and documenting your components.

Research & Gather Notes

- **Official Docs & Blogs**
    - Node.js "Getting Started" guide for your OS.
    - React "Create a New React App" docs (with TypeScript template).
    - Storybook "Installation" tutorial.
- **Community Examples**
    - GitHub repos bootstrapped with CRA + Storybook configuration.
    - CodeSandboxes demonstrating Vite + React + TS + Storybook.
- **Your Own Experience**
    - I prefer Vite for faster hot-reload, but CRA is broadly familiar; we'll show both.

- Pinning your Storybook version prevents unexpected breaking changes mid-book.

Before we dive into component architecture and theming, we need a consistent local environment. Installing the latest LTS of Node.js ensures compatibility with build tools. We'll scaffold a React project configured for TypeScript, then layer in Storybook for interactive component development and documentation. Finally, we'll verify our setup by running both the app and Storybook simultaneously.

Concept Breakdown

- **Node.js & npm**: The JavaScript runtime and package manager that drive your build and dependency workflows.
- **Create React App (CRA) / Vite**: CLI tools that generate a production-ready React project with sensible defaults.
- **TypeScript Configuration**: A `tsconfig.json` file that instructs the compiler on JSX handling, strictness, and module resolution.
- **Storybook CLI**: An interactive development environment for building and testing components in isolation.
- **Monorepo Tools** (optional): Tools like Lerna or Nx for managing multiple packages (e.g., your UI library and your application) in one repo.

Code Walkthrough

```
# 1. Install Node.js (LTS) via https://nodejs.org
node --version
npm --version

# 2a. Scaffold with Create React App (TypeScript template)
npx create-react-app design-system --template typescript
cd design-system

# 2b. OR scaffold with Vite (faster rebuilds)
npm create vite@latest design-system -- --template react-ts
cd design-system

# 3. Install Storybook
npx sb init --builder webpack5

# 4. Update package.json scripts
# ————————————————————————————————————————————————
```

```
# {
#   "scripts": {
#     "start": "react-scripts start",
#     "build": "react-scripts build",
#     "storybook": "start-storybook -p 6006",
#     "build-storybook": "build-storybook"
#   }
# }
```

- **Why each step matters:**
    - **Scaffold**: Generates a working React+TS project with ESLint, Jest, and type definitions.
    - **Storybook**: Installs peer dependencies and sample stories so you can preview components in isolation.
    - **Scripts**: Enables `npm run start` for your app and `npm run storybook` for your component library docs.

Common Pitfalls

1. **Mismatched Node/npm Versions**
    - Older Node versions can break CRA or Storybook.
    - **Fix:** Use an LTS release (e.g. Node 18.x) and upgrade `npm` if needed.
2. **Storybook Dependency Conflicts**
    - Peer-dependency errors when Storybook tries to install its own React.
    - **Fix:** Ensure your React version matches Storybook's required version; pin dependencies in `package.json`.
3. **Missing TypeScript Types**
    - Errors like "Cannot find module '*.png'" or missing `@types/*`.
    - **Fix:** Add `declare module '*.png';` in a `global.d.ts` and install necessary `@types` packages.

```
Environment Setup Checklist
┌──────────────────────────────┐
│ 1. Node.js ≥ 18.x & npm ≥ 8  │
│ 2. React+TypeScript scaffold │
│    • CRA or Vite             │
│ 3. Storybook initialized     │
│    • npx sb init             │
│ 4. Scripts configured        │
│    • npm start               │
│    • npm run storybook       │
└──────────────────────────────┘
```

Hands-On Exercise

Objective: Verify your toolchain and run both the application and Storybook.

1. **Run the App:**

```
npm run start
```

   Confirm the React welcome page renders at `http://localhost:3000`.

2. **Run Storybook:**

```
npm run storybook
```

   Open `http://localhost:6006` and see the default "Button" story.

3. **Deliverable:**
   - A running React app in one terminal.
   - Storybook UI in another terminal, showing at least one story.
   - A screenshot or short video clip demonstrating both.

Key Takeaways

- Your local environment is now configured for TypeScript-based React development.
- Storybook is set up to build and document components in isolation.
- You know where to look for and resolve common setup issues.

Next Steps
Move on to **Chapter 2.1**, where we'll begin building your first design tokens—defining colors, typography, and spacing to form the foundation of your React design system.

Chapter 2: Foundations of a React Design System

2.1 Defining Your Design Tokens: Colors, Typography, Spacing

Goal Statement
In this section you'll learn how to codify your brand's visual language into reusable design tokens—defining color palettes, typographic scales, and spacing units—to serve as the single source of truth for every React component.

Key Terms

- **Design Token**
- **Semantic Naming**
- **Scale**
- **CSS Variables**
- **TypeScript Interface**

Practical Outcome
By the end, you'll be able to create a TypeScript-backed token file (and corresponding CSS variables) that defines your colors, font sizes, and spacing scale, and import those tokens into your React components with full type safety.

Research & Gather Notes

- **Official Docs & Blogs**
    - Salesforce's Lightning Design System token methodology.
    - CSS-Tricks article on "Design Tokens in Practice."
- **Community Examples**
    - GitHub: Shopify Polaris tokens defined in JSON and generated to CSS/TypeScript.
    - CodeSandbox: "tokens-to-theme" generator demos.
- **Your Own Experience**

- Found that using semantic names (`--color-primary`, `--spacing-2`) avoids hard-to-maintain literal values in components.
- Learned that exporting tokens as both CSS variables and TS constants ensures consistency across styling and logic.

At the heart of every design system lies its **design tokens**—the smallest, most atomic style values that represent your brand's look and feel. Rather than scattering raw color codes, pixel values, or font arrays throughout your codebase, tokens allow you to centralize these definitions and refer to them semantically. When the brand color changes or the spacing scale needs adjustment, you update one source and every component adapts instantly.

Tokens typically fall into categories—colors, typography, spacing, shadows, and more—but in this section we'll focus on the core three: your color palette, your typographic scale, and your spacing units. We'll define tokens in a dual format: CSS custom properties (for styling) and a TypeScript object (for build-time safety). This approach ensures that whether you're writing styled-components, Tailwind plugins, or plain CSS, you have a consistent, type-checked reference for every style value.

Concept Breakdown

1. **Design Token**
   - A named variable representing a single design value (e.g. `#0055FF` → `color-primary`).
   - Acts as the "truth" for that style attribute.
2. **Semantic Naming**
   - Naming tokens by intent (e.g. `color-success` vs. `#28A745`) makes code more readable and maintainable.
3. **Scale**
   - A consistent progression of values (e.g. font sizes `[12, 14, 16, 20, 24]` or spacing `[4, 8, 16, 32]`).
   - Ensures visual rhythm and hierarchy.
4. **CSS Variables**
   - Exposed at runtime (`--spacing-2: 8px;`) so your stylesheets can consume tokens directly.
5. **TypeScript Interface**
   - A build-time construct that enforces correct token usage in code (`tokens.spacing[2]`).

Code Walkthrough

```
/* src/styles/tokens.css */
:root {
  /* Color Palette */
  --color-primary: #0055FF;
  --color-secondary: #FF5500;
  --color-success: #28A745;
  --color-text: #333333;

  /* Typography Scale */
  --font-size-0: 12px;
  --font-size-1: 14px;
  --font-size-2: 16px;
  --font-size-3: 20px;
  --font-size-4: 24px;

  /* Spacing Scale */
  --spacing-0: 4px;
  --spacing-1: 8px;
  --spacing-2: 16px;
  --spacing-3: 32px;
}
// src/styles/tokens.ts
export interface Tokens {
  color: Record<'primary' | 'secondary' | 'success' | 'text',
string>;
  fontSize: Record<0 | 1 | 2 | 3 | 4, string>;
  spacing: Record<0 | 1 | 2 | 3, string>;
}

export const tokens: Tokens = {
  color: {
    primary: 'var(--color-primary)',
    secondary: 'var(--color-secondary)',
    success: 'var(--color-success)',
    text: 'var(--color-text)',
  },
  fontSize: {
    0: 'var(--font-size-0)',
    1: 'var(--font-size-1)',
    2: 'var(--font-size-2)',
    3: 'var(--font-size-3)',
    4: 'var(--font-size-4)',
  },
  spacing: {
    0: 'var(--spacing-0)',
    1: 'var(--spacing-1)',
    2: 'var(--spacing-2)',
    3: 'var(--spacing-3)',
  },
```

```
};
```

- **What it does:**
  - Defines tokens once in CSS, then references them via TypeScript for safe usage in JS/TS code.
- **Why this approach:**
  - **Runtime flexibility:** CSS variables allow dynamic theming (dark mode, user overrides).
  - **Type safety:** TypeScript interface prevents typos and ensures only valid token keys are used.

Common Pitfalls

1. **Hard-Coded Fallbacks**
   - Using raw values instead of `var(...)` leads to drift.
   - **Fix:** Always reference tokens via `var(--…)` or the TS `tokens` object.
2. **Inconsistent Scales**
   - Mixing pixel-based and rem-based values without a clear scale.
   - **Fix:** Decide on one unit (px or rem) and stick to it across tokens.
3. **Over-Generalizing Names**
   - Naming everything "primary" when multiple variants exist.
   - **Fix:** Reserve "primary" for your main brand accent; use semantic intent (e.g., "success," "warning").

Design Token Mapping Table

Token Category	Token	Value
Color	primary	#0055FF
Color	secondary	#FF5500
Font Size	2	16px
Spacing	1	8px

Hands-On Exercise

Objective: Create and consume your own design tokens.

1. **Define Tokens:**

   - Copy the CSS and TS token declarations above into your project under `src/styles/`.
2. **Consume Tokens:**
   - In a new component (e.g., `<Card>`), apply `tokens.spacing[2]` for padding and `tokens.color.text` for text color.
3. **Verify:**
   - Run the app and confirm the styles reflect your token values.
4. **Deliverable:**
   - A `<Card>` component file and a screenshot showing correct spacing and color.

Key Takeaways

- Design tokens centralize your core style values for colors, typography, and spacing.
- Dual definitions (CSS variables + TypeScript) combine runtime flexibility with type safety.
- Semantic naming and consistent scales ensure a coherent look and facilitate theming.

Next Steps
Continue to **Section 2.2**, where we'll establish naming conventions and folder structure to organize these tokens and components for maximum clarity and scalability.

2.2 Establishing Naming Conventions and Folder Structure

Goal Statement
In this section you'll learn how to define clear, semantic naming conventions for components and tokens, and organize your files and folders so that your React design system scales predictably as it grows.

Key Terms

- **Semantic Naming**
- **Folder Hierarchy**
- **Barrel Files**

- **Atomic Grouping**
- **Feature Modules**

Practical Outcome
By the end, you'll be able to create a standardized folder layout for your design system, apply consistent file and directory names, and leverage barrel exports so that consuming code imports components predictably.

Research & Gather Notes

- **Official Docs & Blogs**
  - React "Folder Structure" best practices from the React docs.
  - Brad Frost's Atomic Design folder organization recommendations.
- **Community Examples**
  - GitHub: Shopify Polaris monorepo structure.
  - GitHub: Atlassian's `atlaskit` component grouping by package.
- **Your Own Experience**
  - Noted that inconsistent file names (camelCase vs. kebab-case) cause import errors.
  - Found barrel files (index.ts) simplify imports and reduce path complexity.

A robust design system begins not only with well-defined tokens, but also with a directory structure and naming scheme that developers can intuitively follow. Without conventions, teams quickly diverge—some files in `PascalCase`, others in `kebab-case`; some components tucked under "ui/Buttons," others scattered in "components/Buttons." The result is confusion, merge conflicts, and import headaches.

To prevent this, we'll adopt a folder hierarchy influenced by Atomic Design and feature-based modules. Each component lives in its own folder named in PascalCase (matching the component's name), containing its implementation file, styles, tests, and documentation. Barrel files (`index.ts`) at each level export these modules, enabling clean imports like `import { Button } from '@my-org/design-system';` regardless of the underlying path depth.

Concept Breakdown

1. **Semantic Naming**
   - Component folders and files use PascalCase (`Button/Button.tsx`).
   - Tokens and utilities use kebab-case for CSS (`tokens.css`) and camelCase for JS exports (`tokens.ts`).
2. **Folder Hierarchy**
   - Top-level `src/components/` for your React components.
   - Group by "atomic" level or feature, e.g. `atoms/`, `molecules/`, `organisms/`.
   - Parallel `src/styles/` for tokens and theming.
3. **Barrel Files**
   - Each folder contains an `index.ts` that re-exports its modules.
   - Consumers import from the folder root, e.g. `import { Card } from 'components/molecules';`.
4. **Atomic Grouping vs. Feature Modules**
   - **Atomic Grouping:** Organize by component granularity (small → large).
   - **Feature Modules:** Group components by feature or domain (e.g., `profile/`, `dashboard/`) when atomic grouping becomes overly granular.
5. **Consistency Enforcement**
   - Use lint rules (`eslint-plugin-filenames`) and commit hooks to enforce naming.
   - Document conventions in a `CONTRIBUTING.md`.

Code Walkthrough

```
design-system/
├── src/
│   ├── components/
│   │   ├── atoms/
│   │   │   ├── Button/
│   │   │   │   ├── Button.tsx
│   │   │   │   ├── Button.css
│   │   │   │   ├── Button.test.tsx
│   │   │   │   └── index.ts
│   │   │   └── index.ts
│   │   ├── molecules/
│   │   │   ├── Card/
│   │   │   │   ├── Card.tsx
│   │   │   │   ├── Card.css
│   │   │   │   └── index.ts
```

```
│   │   │   └── index.ts
│   │   └── index.ts
│   ├── styles/
│   │   ├── tokens.css
│   │   ├── tokens.ts
│   │   └── index.ts
│   └── index.ts
└── package.json
```

In `src/components/atoms/Button/index.ts`:

```
export { Button } from './Button';
```

In `src/components/atoms/index.ts`:

```
export * from './Button';
```

In `src/components/index.ts`:

```
export * from './atoms';
export * from './molecules';
```

- **What it does:**
    - Creates a flattened import surface.
    - Hides folder complexity behind barrel exports.
- **Why this approach:**
    - **Discoverability:** Developers find components via predictable paths.
    - **Maintainability:** Renaming a folder or moving a file doesn't break imports across the codebase.

Common Pitfalls

1. **Deep Import Paths**
    - Avoid imports like `import Button from 'components/atoms/Button/Button';`.
    - **Fix:** Always use barrel exports (`import { Button } from 'components';`).
2. **Inconsistent Casing**
    - Mixing file casing leads to errors on case-sensitive file systems.
    - **Fix:** Enforce PascalCase for component folders/files, kebab-case for style and utility filenames.
3. **Over-Nesting**

- Too many folder levels can make navigation cumbersome.
- **Fix:** Limit nesting to two levels deep (e.g. `atoms/Button`) and use feature modules when necessary.

```
Folder Structure Overview
┌ src/
│
├─ components/
│   ├─ atoms/
│   │   └─ Button/
│   │       ├ Button.tsx
│   │       └ index.ts
│   └─ molecules/
│       └─ Card/
│           ├ Card.tsx
│           └ index.ts
│
└─ styles/
    ├ tokens.css
    └ tokens.ts
```

Hands-On Exercise

Objective: Implement and export a new "Badge" component following conventions.

1. **Create Folder:**
   - `src/components/atoms/Badge/`
2. **Add Files:**
   - `Badge.tsx` (component implementation)
   - `Badge.css` (styles)
   - `Badge.test.tsx` (unit tests)
   - `index.ts` (barrel export)
3. **Update Parent Barrel:**
   - Add `export * from './Badge';` in `src/components/atoms/index.ts`.
4. **Verify Imports:**
   - In `App.tsx`, import with `import { Badge } from 'components';` and render it.
5. **Deliverable:**
   - Folder structure snapshot and a screenshot of the running Badge in your app.

Key Takeaways

- Semantic, consistent naming and folder layouts prevent confusion and import errors.
- Barrel files flatten your import paths and abstract folder depth.
- Enforcing conventions via lint rules and documentation keeps the codebase uniform.

Next Steps
Proceed to **Section 2.3**, where we'll choose a styling strategy—comparing CSS-in-JS, utility-first, and plain CSS—to apply on top of this solid structure.

2.3 Choosing a Styling Strategy (CSS-in-JS, Utility-First, or Plain CSS)

Goal Statement
In this section you'll compare three dominant styling approaches for React design systems—CSS-in-JS, utility-first CSS, and plain CSS modules—to choose the strategy that best balances maintainability, performance, and team familiarity.

Key Terms

- **CSS-in-JS**
- **Utility-First CSS**
- **CSS Modules**
- **Dead Code Elimination**
- **Theming**

Practical Outcome
By the end, you'll be able to weigh pros and cons of each approach, configure a minimal example for your preferred strategy, and document the rationale for your choice in your design-system README.

Research & Gather Notes

- **Official Docs & Blogs**
    - Emotion & styled-components documentation on CSS-in-JS patterns.
    - Tailwind CSS guide on utility-first design and purge-CSS for bundle optimization.
    - CSS Modules overview from the Create React App docs.
- **Community Examples**
    - GitHub: `chakra-ui/chakra-ui` (CSS-in-JS with system props).
    - GitHub: `tailwindlabs/tailwindcss` example projects.
    - CodeSandbox: demo repos showing CSS Modules in React.
- **Your Own Experience**
    - Noticed CSS-in-JS makes theming trivial but can increase bundle size if not configured for dead-code elimination.
    - Found utility-first fosters consistency but can clutter JSX if over-applied.
    - Plain CSS Modules offer a familiar workflow but require naming discipline to avoid global leakage.

Selecting the right styling strategy is pivotal for a robust design system. **CSS-in-JS** libraries (e.g., Emotion, styled-components) let you colocate styles with components and leverage JavaScript logic for dynamic theming. **Utility-first CSS** (e.g., Tailwind CSS) provides atomic classes that encourage reuse and eliminate custom CSS, but can lead to verbose JSX. **Plain CSS Modules** strike a middle ground: styles are isolated by default, preserving familiar CSS syntax while avoiding global collisions.

Each approach comes with trade-offs. CSS-in-JS often simplifies theming—switching a color token changes all styled components at runtime—but you must configure Babel or bundler plugins to tree-shake unused styles. Utility-first gives you a highly predictable design language via classes like `p-4` or `text-gray-700`, yet teams can become overwhelmed by long class lists. CSS Modules require maintaining separate `.module.css` files, but benefit from static analysis and straightforward build integration.

Concept Breakdown

1. **CSS-in-JS**
    - Styles written in JavaScript (template literals or object syntax).
    - Pros: dynamic theming, scoped by default, familiar JS API.
    - Cons: runtime cost, larger bundle if not optimized.

2. **Utility-First CSS**
   - Predefined classes for every atomic style.
   - Pros: no custom CSS, consistent spacing/color scales, small final CSS via purge.
   - Cons: verbose markup, learning curve for class names.
3. **Plain CSS Modules**
   - CSS files with hashed class names automatically scoped to components.
   - Pros: separate style files, native CSS syntax, zero-runtime overhead.
   - Cons: less dynamic theming, potential duplication of common styles.
4. **Dead Code Elimination**
   - Build-time process that removes unused CSS or styled-component rules.
   - Essential for CSS-in-JS and utility-first to minimize bundle size.
5. **Theming**
   - Mechanism to switch color palettes or spacing scales at runtime.
   - CSS-in-JS can leverage context; utility-first may require custom configuration.

Code Walkthrough

CSS-in-JS (Emotion) Example:

```
/** Button.tsx **/
/** @jsxImportSource @emotion/react */
import { css } from '@emotion/react'

const buttonStyle = (primary) => css`
  padding: 0.5rem 1rem;
  background: ${primary ? 'var(--color-primary)' : 'var(--
color-secondary)'};
  color: white;
`

export function Button({ primary, children }) {
  return <button
css={buttonStyle(primary)}>{children}</button>
}
```

Utility-First (Tailwind) Example:

```
// Button.tsx
export function Button({ primary, children }) {
  const base = 'px-4 py-2 font-semibold rounded'
  const variant = primary ? 'bg-blue-600 text-white' : 'bg-
gray-200 text-gray-800'
  return <button className={`${base}
${variant}`}>{children}</button>
}
```

CSS Modules Example:

```
/* Button.module.css */
.button {
  padding: 0.5rem 1rem;
  border-radius: 0.25rem;
}
.primary {
  background: var(--color-primary);
  color: white;
}
.secondary {
  background: var(--color-secondary);
  color: #333;
}
// Button.tsx
import styles from './Button.module.css'

export function Button({ primary, children }) {
  const variant = primary ? styles.primary : styles.secondary
  return <button className={`${styles.button}
${variant}`}>{children}</button>
}
```

Common Pitfalls

1. **Unoptimized CSS-in-JS Bundles**
   - Forgetting to enable Babel plugin for source extraction leads to huge runtime styles.
   - **Fix:** Add `@emotion/babel-plugin` or `styled-components` Babel macro.
2. **Excessive Utility Classes**
   - JSX becomes cluttered and hard to read.
   - **Fix:** Create component wrappers or use `clsx` to conditionally apply utilities.
3. **Global Leakage in CSS Modules**
   - Forgetting `.module` suffix exposes classes globally.

- **Fix:** Enforce naming convention and configure webpack to treat only `*.module.css` as modules.

Styling Strategy Comparison

Approach	Theming	Bundle Impact	Syntax Style
CSS-in-JS	Runtime via JS	Medium-Large	JS-template
Utility-First	Config only	Small	Class names
CSS Modules	Build-time	Small	CSS files

Hands-On Exercise

Objective: Set up all three strategies in a single project and compare bundle sizes.

1. **Scaffold Three Folders:**
   - `src/cssinjs/`, `src/tailwind/`, `src/cssmodules/`.
2. **Implement `<Button>` in Each:**
   - Use Emotion in `cssinjs`, Tailwind in `tailwind`, CSS Modules in `cssmodules`.
3. **Build & Analyze:**
   - Run production builds (`npm run build`) for each folder.
   - Use `source-map-explorer` or similar to report final CSS/JS sizes.
4. **Deliverable:**
   - A table listing each folder and its bundle size.
   - A brief note on which strategy you'd choose and why.

Key Takeaways

- CSS-in-JS excels at dynamic theming but requires optimization.
- Utility-first enforces a consistent design language with minimal custom CSS.
- CSS Modules balance familiarity and scoping with zero runtime overhead.

Next Steps
Proceed to **Section 2.4**, where we'll integrate TypeScript to enforce token usage and further tighten your styling workflow.

2.4 Integrating TypeScript for Type-Safe Tokens

Goal Statement
In this section you'll learn how to leverage TypeScript interfaces and utility types to ensure that your React components only consume valid design tokens—preventing typos and mismatches at compile time.

Key Terms

- **TypeScript Interface**
- **Literal Types**
- **Mapped Types**
- **Compile-Time Safety**
- **Token Namespace**

Practical Outcome
By the end, you'll have a `.ts` token definition that mirrors your CSS variables, complete with strong typing so that attempts to reference an undefined token produce a compiler error.

Research & Gather Notes

- **Official Docs & Blogs**
    - TypeScript handbook: "Literal Types & Union Types" and "Mapped Types."
    - CSS-in-TypeScript patterns from Microsoft's Fluent UI.
- **Community Examples**
    - GitHub: Shopify Polaris' `tokens.ts` exports with `as const`.
    - GitHub: Atlassian's `@atlaskit/tokens` implementation.
- **Your Own Experience**
    - Found that using `as const` on token objects preserves literal types and enables exhaustive switch statements.

- Learned to generate TS token definitions automatically from a JSON source to avoid duplication.

When styling large applications, it's all too easy to mistype a token name—`primary` vs. `priamry`—and only discover the UI error at runtime. By integrating TypeScript, we can catch these mistakes at compile time. We'll define our tokens in a `.ts` file using `as const` to produce literal types, then derive TypeScript interfaces that represent the valid keys for colors, spacing, and font sizes.

This type-safe layer not only prevents errors, but also powers IDE autocompletion, making the developer experience frictionless. As your token set evolves—adding new colors or renaming spacing steps—TypeScript will flag any component that needs updating. The result is a rock-solid bridge between your design language and your React code.

Concept Breakdown

1. **TypeScript Interface & `as const`**
   - Using `const tokens = { … } as const` locks the object's values and key names into literal types.
2. **Literal & Union Types**
   - Extracting `keyof typeof tokens.color` produces a union of valid color names (`"primary" | "secondary" | …`).
3. **Mapped Types**
   - Constructing types like `Record<keyof typeof tokens.color, string>` ensures every token key maps to a string value.
4. **Compile-Time Safety**
   - References to tokens outside the defined union cause TypeScript errors before you even run the app.
5. **Token Namespace**
   - Grouping tokens under namespaces (`tokens.color`, `tokens.spacing`) keeps imports organized and type definitions clear.

Code Walkthrough

```
// src/styles/tokens.ts
export const tokens = {
```

```
  color: {
    primary: 'var(--color-primary)',
    secondary: 'var(--color-secondary)',
    success: 'var(--color-success)',
    text: 'var(--color-text)',
  },
  spacing: {
    small: 'var(--spacing-1)',
    medium: 'var(--spacing-2)',
    large: 'var(--spacing-3)',
  },
  fontSize: {
    body: 'var(--font-size-2)',
    heading: 'var(--font-size-4)',
  },
} as const;

// Derive types
export type ColorToken    = keyof typeof tokens.color;    //
"primary" | "secondary" | "success" | "text"
export type SpacingToken  = keyof typeof tokens.spacing;  //
"small" | "medium" | "large"
export type FontSizeToken = keyof typeof tokens.fontSize; //
"body" | "heading"

// Helper type for component props
interface BoxProps {
  padding: SpacingToken;
  color: ColorToken;
  fontSize: FontSizeToken;
}

export function Box({ padding, color, fontSize }: BoxProps) {
  return (
    <div
      style={{
        padding: tokens.spacing[padding],
        color: tokens.color[color],
        fontSize: tokens.fontSize[fontSize],
      }}
    />
  );
}
```

- **What it does:**
  - Defines `tokens` with `as const` to preserve literal keys.
  - Extracts union types for each token category.
  - Uses those types in `BoxProps` so invalid token names error out at compile time.

- **Why this approach:**
  - **Type Safety:** Prevents typos and enforces consistency.
  - **Developer Ergonomics:** Auto-completion in editors surfaces valid token names.
  - **Maintainability:** Adding or removing tokens updates both JS and TS layers automatically.

Common Pitfalls

1. **Forgetting `as const`**
   - Without it, TypeScript widens types to `string`, losing literal key safety.
   - **Fix:** Always append `as const` when exporting the token object.
2. **Manual Duplication**
   - Maintaining separate JSON and TS token definitions leads to drift.
   - **Fix:** Generate TS from a single JSON or CSS-vars source wherever possible.
3. **Overly Broad Types**
   - Using `string` instead of `keyof typeof tokens.color` negates safety.
   - **Fix:** Rely on derived union types for all token-based props.

```
Token Type Extraction
┌────────────────────────┐
│ const tokens = {...}   │   as const
└───────────┬────────────┘
            ▼
┌──────────────────────────────┐
│ type ColorToken = keyof      │
│  typeof tokens.color         │
│  => "primary" | "secondary"  │
└──────────────────────────────┘
```

Hands-On Exercise

Objective: Enforce type-safe usage of tokens in a new component.

1. **Extend Tokens:**
   - Add a new `warning` color and `xlarge` spacing to `tokens.ts`.
2. **Consume in Props:**

    - Create a `Banner` component that accepts `color: ColorToken` and `padding: SpacingToken`.
3. **Test Safety:**
    - Attempt to use an invalid token (e.g. `color="alert"`) and confirm TypeScript errors.
4. **Deliverable:**
    - Updated `tokens.ts`, `Banner.tsx`, and a screenshot of your IDE showing auto-completion and a deliberate error.

Key Takeaways

- Using `as const` locks token keys for literal type extraction.
- Union types (`keyof typeof tokens.*`) guarantee compile-time safety.
- Integrating tokens into component props enforces consistent design usage.

Next Steps
Proceed to **Chapter 3.1**, where we'll begin building the first core components—starting with buttons and form controls that consume these type-safe tokens.

Tokens → CSS Variable Mapping Table

Design Token → CSS Variable Mapping Table

Token	CSS Variable
color.primary	--color-primary
color.secondary	--color-secondary
color.success	--color-success
color.text	--color-text
fontSize.0	--font-size-0
fontSize.1	--font-size-1
fontSize.2	--font-size-2
fontSize.3	--font-size-3
fontSize.4	--font-size-4
spacing.0	--spacing-0
spacing.1	--spacing-1
spacing.2	--spacing-2

spacing.3	--spacing-3

2.5 End-of-Chapter Summary & Key Takeaways

1. **Token Centralization:**
   - Design tokens (colors, typography, spacing) serve as the single source of truth for your system.
   - Defining them once—in CSS variables and a TypeScript object—prevents scattered magic values.
2. **Semantic, Consistent Naming:**
   - Use clear, intent-driven names (`primary`, `success`, `spacing-2`) to enhance readability.
   - Dual definitions (CSS custom properties + TS literal types) ensure both runtime flexibility and compile-time safety.
3. **Folder Structure & Conventions:**
   - Organize components and styles with PascalCase folders and barrel `index.ts` files.
   - Enforce naming and import consistency via lint rules and documentation.
4. **Styling Strategy Trade-Offs:**
   - **CSS-in-JS:** Great for dynamic theming, requires bundler optimization.
   - **Utility-First:** Ensures uniform atomic classes, can clutter JSX.
   - **CSS Modules:** Familiar CSS syntax with auto-scoped classes, less dynamic.
5. **Type-Safe Token Integration:**
   - Leverage `as const` and `keyof typeof` to derive literal union types.
   - Component props typed with these unions catch invalid token references at compile time.

With these foundations in place—centralized tokens, clear structure, a chosen styling approach, and type safety—you're ready to start building real React components in Chapter 3.

2.6 Hands-On Exercises

Exercise 1: Centralize Your Tokens

- **Objective:** Create and verify your CSS and TypeScript token definitions.
- **Steps:**
  1. In `src/styles/`, add `tokens.css` with your color, typography, and spacing variables.
  2. Add `tokens.ts` exporting the same values under `as const`.
  3. Import `tokens` in a simple component (e.g. `<div style={{ color: tokens.color.primary }}>`) and confirm the CSS variable resolves at runtime.
- **Deliverable:** The two token files plus a screenshot of a component rendering with your primary color and spacing tokens applied.

Exercise 2: Enforce Your Folder & Naming Conventions

- **Objective:** Scaffold a component folder structure and use barrel exports.
- **Steps:**
  1. Under `src/components/`, create `atoms/Button/` and `molecules/Card/` folders.
  2. In each, add a stub `ComponentName.tsx`, `ComponentName.css`, `ComponentName.test.tsx`, and `index.ts` exporting the component.
  3. In `src/components/index.ts`, re-export both `Button` and `Card`.
  4. In `App.tsx`, import them via `import { Button, Card } from 'components';` and render each.
- **Deliverable:** A directory tree screenshot and a running view showing both components in your app.

Exercise 3: Compare Styling Strategies

- **Objective:** Evaluate CSS-in-JS, utility-first, and CSS Modules by implementing the same component three ways.
- **Steps:**
  1. Create three variants of `Badge`:
     - `src/cssinjs/Badge.tsx` using Emotion or styled-components.
     - `src/tailwind/Badge.tsx` with Tailwind utility classes.
     - `src/cssmodules/Badge.module.css` + `Badge.tsx` consuming it.
  2. Build each variant in isolation (`npm run build`) and measure CSS/JS output size (e.g. via `source-map-explorer`).
  3. Note any differences in code verbosity and bundle impact.
- **Deliverable:**
  - A table listing each variant, its approximate bundle size, and a one-sentence pros/cons summary for each approach.

2.7 Next Steps: Token-Driven Theming

In this section you'll learn how to leverage your centralized design tokens to implement runtime theming—switching palettes or spacing scales on the fly—so that your React app can adapt to light/dark modes or custom brand themes with minimal code changes.

Key Terms

- **Theme Context**
- **CSS Custom Properties**
- **Theme Provider**
- **Dynamic Token Overrides**
- **React Context API**

Practical Outcome
By the end, you'll be able to build a `<ThemeProvider>` component that injects different token sets (colors, spacing, typography) via CSS variables

and React context, and consume those tokens seamlessly in your components.

Research & Gather Notes

- **Official Docs & Blogs**
  - React "Context" documentation for global state.
  - CSS Tricks article on "Dark Mode with CSS Variables."
- **Community Examples**
  - GitHub: Chakra UI's theming implementation.
  - GitHub: Tailwind's custom themes via CSS variables and `<script>`.
- **Your Own Experience**
  - Found that toggling a CSS class on `<html>` with a separate token file for dark mode simplifies overrides.
  - Learned to combine React context for logical theme value and CSS variables for style injection.

Once your tokens are defined and centralized, the next step is to enable **dynamic theming**—letting users switch between light and dark modes, brand variants, or accessibility-focused high-contrast palettes. By driving your CSS variables from a React Context-based `<ThemeProvider>`, you can update your entire application's look by simply toggling a theme key.

Concept Breakdown

1. **Theme Context**
   - A React Context that holds the current theme key (e.g., `'light' | 'dark'`).
   - Provides a `toggleTheme` function to switch values.
2. **CSS Custom Properties**
   - Each theme has its own token file: `tokens.light.css` and `tokens.dark.css`.
   - Applying one set of variables at the root overrides the default.
3. **Theme Provider**
   - Wraps your app, reads the theme key from context, and adds the appropriate CSS class to `<body>` or `<html>`.

4. **Dynamic Token Overrides**
   - Because tokens are CSS variables, new values take effect immediately without reloading or remounting components.
5. **React Context API**
   - Enables any component to read `useTheme()` for the current theme and call `toggleTheme()`.

Code Walkthrough

```
// src/theme/ThemeContext.tsx
import React, { createContext, useContext, useState,
useEffect } from 'react';

type Theme = 'light' | 'dark';
const ThemeContext = createContext<{ theme: Theme; toggle: ()
=> void }>({
  theme: 'light',
  toggle: () => {},
});

export function ThemeProvider({ children }: { children:
React.ReactNode }) {
  const [theme, setTheme] = useState<Theme>('light');

  useEffect(() => {
    document.documentElement.className = theme; // toggles
.light or .dark on <html>
  }, [theme]);

  const toggle = () => setTheme((prev) => (prev === 'light' ?
'dark' : 'light'));

  return (
    <ThemeContext.Provider value={{ theme, toggle }}>
      {children}
    </ThemeContext.Provider>
  );
}

export const useTheme = () => useContext(ThemeContext);
/* src/styles/tokens.light.css */
:root.light {
  --color-primary: #0055FF;
  --color-text: #333;
  /* …other light tokens… */
}
```

```css
/* src/styles/tokens.dark.css */
:root.dark {
  --color-primary: #66B2FF;
  --color-text: #EEE;
  /* …other dark tokens… */
}
```

- **What it does:**
    - Adds the theme name as a class on `<html>`, causing the corresponding CSS file's variables to apply.
    - Provides `useTheme()` for components to read and toggle the theme.
- **Why this approach:**
    - **Immediate updates:** CSS variables react to class changes instantly.
    - **Minimal re-renders:** Only the context state changes; styled components and CSS variables handle the rest.

Common Pitfalls

1. **Flicker on Initial Load**
    - Theme toggles before CSS loads, causing a flash of default theme.
    - **Fix:** Persist theme in `localStorage` and apply class in a small inline `<script>` before React hydrates.
2. **Incomplete Overrides**
    - Forgetting to include all tokens in the alternate CSS file results in mixed styles.
    - **Fix:** Use a CSS preprocessor or token generator to ensure both theme files have identical variable sets.
3. **Context Misuse**
    - Over-subscribing many components to context can hurt performance.
    - **Fix:** Use context only for theme toggling; let CSS variables handle style updates.

```
ThemeProvider Flowchart

┌──────────────────────┐
│  App Root            │
│ <ThemeProvider>      │
└──────────┬───────────┘
           │
     ┌─────▼─────┐
     │ useState  │
     │ theme     │
```

```
 └──────────┬──────────┘
            │
 ┌──────────▼──────────────┐
 │ <html className=        │
 │   theme>                │
 └──────────┬──────────────┘
            │
┌───────────▼──────────────┐
│ CSS tokens.{theme}.css   │
│ defines vars             │
└──────────────────────────┘
```

Hands-On Exercise

Objective: Implement theme persistence and toggle UI.

1. **Persist Theme:**
   - Read `localStorage.theme` in `ThemeProvider`'s initial `useState`.
   - Update `localStorage` whenever `theme` changes.
2. **Build Toggle Button:**
   - Create a `<ThemeToggle>` component using `useTheme()`.
   - Render a button that calls `toggle()` and displays the current theme icon.
3. **Verify:**
   - Reload the page—theme choice should persist.
   - Toggle and observe CSS variable changes in real time.
4. **Deliverable:**
   - Updated `ThemeProvider.tsx`, new `ThemeToggle.tsx`, and a short screencast showing persistence across reloads.

Key Takeaways

- Runtime theming uses CSS classes and CSS variables for instant visual updates.
- React Context provides the logical theme state and toggle function.
- Persisting the theme and a preload script prevent flashes of unstyled content.

Next Steps
Proceed to **Chapter 3.1**, where we'll start implementing core components—beginning with buttons that automatically inherit your token-driven theming.

Chapter 3: Building Core Components

3.1 Buttons, Inputs, and Form Controls

In this section you'll learn how to build foundational form controls—buttons, text inputs, and checkboxes—as reusable, accessible React components that consume your design tokens and styling strategy.

Key Terms

- **Controlled vs. Uncontrolled Components**
- **ARIA Attributes**
- **Form State Management**
- **Component Variants**
- **Token Consumption**

Practical Outcome
By the end, you'll implement `<Button>`, `<TextInput>`, and `<Checkbox>` components that accept props for variant, size, and state, apply your tokens for styling, and expose a clean API for form composition.

Research & Gather Notes

- **Official Docs & Blogs**
  - React docs: "Forms" guide on controlled components.
  - MDN: Accessibility fundamentals for form controls (focus, labels, ARIA).
- **Community Examples**
  - GitHub: Chakra UI's source for Button and Input.
  - GitHub: Reach UI's accessible form primitives.
- **Your Own Experience**
  - Found that using `forwardRef` on form controls simplifies focus management.
  - Learned to expose an `isDisabled` prop that disables pointer events and sets `aria-disabled`.

Buttons and inputs are the cornerstone of any UI. A robust design system requires these elements to be both visually consistent and behaviorally reliable. In React, form controls are most useful when they integrate seamlessly with application state and accessibility standards. By building custom `<Button>`, `<TextInput>`, and `<Checkbox>` components, you ensure every part of your UI adheres to your design tokens, supports theming, and remains accessible out of the box.

We'll start with `<Button>`, supporting `variant` (primary, secondary), `size` (small, medium, large), and disabled state. Next, we'll create `<TextInput>` with support for `label`, `placeholder`, and error states, wiring it as a controlled component. Finally, we'll implement `<Checkbox>` with proper ARIA roles and keyboard interaction. Throughout, we'll consume `tokens.color`, `tokens.spacing`, and our chosen styling strategy to keep these primitives in sync with the rest of your design system.

Concept Breakdown

1. **Controlled vs. Uncontrolled**
   - **Controlled:** Parent holds `value` and `onChange`, ensuring single source of truth.
   - **Uncontrolled:** Component manages its own state via refs—less predictable for complex forms.
2. **ARIA Attributes**
   - Use `aria-disabled`, `aria-invalid`, and `aria-labelledby` to communicate state to assistive tech.
3. **Component Variants & Sizes**
   - Expose props (`variant`, `size`) that map to specific token combinations for colors and spacing.
4. **Token Consumption**
   - Apply `tokens.color.primary` or `tokens.spacing[2]` in styles or class names, ensuring consistency.
5. **Ref Forwarding**
   - Use `React.forwardRef` so parent forms can imperatively focus or validate controls.

Code Walkthrough

```
// src/components/atoms/Button/Button.tsx
import React, { forwardRef } from 'react';
```

```
import { tokens } from '../../styles/tokens';
import styles from './Button.module.css';

export type ButtonVariant = 'primary' | 'secondary';
export type ButtonSize    = 'small' | 'medium' | 'large';

export interface ButtonProps extends
React.ButtonHTMLAttributes<HTMLButtonElement> {
  variant?: ButtonVariant;
  size?: ButtonSize;
}

export const Button = forwardRef<HTMLButtonElement,
ButtonProps>(
  ({ variant = 'primary', size = 'medium', disabled = false,
children, ...rest }, ref) => {
    const classNames = [
      styles.button,
      styles[variant],
      styles[size],
      disabled && styles.disabled,
    ]
      .filter(Boolean)
      .join(' ');

    return (
      <button
        ref={ref}
        className={classNames}
        disabled={disabled}
        aria-disabled={disabled}
        {...rest}
      >
        {children}
      </button>
    );
  }
);
/* src/components/atoms/Button/Button.module.css */
.button {
  border: none;
  border-radius: 4px;
  cursor: pointer;
  font-weight: 600;
}
.primary {
  background: var(--color-primary);
  color: white;
}
.secondary {
  background: var(--color-secondary);
```

```
  color: white;
}
.small {
  padding: var(--spacing-0) var(--spacing-1);
  font-size: var(--font-size-1);
}
.medium {
  padding: var(--spacing-1) var(--spacing-2);
  font-size: var(--font-size-2);
}
.large {
  padding: var(--spacing-2) var(--spacing-3);
  font-size: var(--font-size-3);
}
.disabled {
  background: #ccc;
  cursor: not-allowed;
}
```

- **What it does:**
  - Defines a variant- and size-aware button, forwarding refs and ARIA attributes.
  - Applies CSS Modules consuming your CSS variable tokens.
- **Why this approach:**
  - **Consistency:** All buttons share the same token-driven styling.
  - **Accessibility:** `disabled` and `aria-disabled` ensure assistive tech understands state.
  - **Flexibility:** Consumers can pass additional HTML attributes (e.g. `onClick`, `type`).

Common Pitfalls

1. **Omitting `type` Attribute**
   - Default `<button>` inside forms can submit unexpectedly.
   - **Fix:** Always set `type="button"` for non-submit buttons, or expose `type` prop.
2. **Not Forwarding Refs**
   - Parent forms can't focus or measure components.
   - **Fix:** Wrap component in `forwardRef` and pass `ref` to underlying element.
3. **Hard-Coded Styles**
   - Embedding literal values instead of tokens leads to drift.
   - **Fix:** Reference CSS variables or TS tokens exclusively.

`<Button>` Variant & Size Mapping

Prop	Options	Resulting Styles
variant	`primary`	`background: var(--color-primary); color: white`
	`secondary`	`background: var(--color-secondary); color: white`
size	`small`	`padding: 4px 8px; font-size: 14px`
	`medium`	`padding: 8px 16px; font-size: 16px`
	`large`	`padding: 16px 32px; font-size: 20px`
disabled	`true`	`background: #ccc; cursor: not-allowed; opacity: 0.6`

Hands-On Exercise

Objective: Build and use `<TextInput>` and `<Checkbox>` alongside `<Button>`.

1. **TextInput:**
   - Create `TextInput.tsx` forwarding a `<input type="text">`, accepting `label`, `value`, `onChange`, and `error` props.
   - Apply tokens for padding, border color, and font size; reflect `error` state with `--color-secondary`.
2. **Checkbox:**
   - Create `Checkbox.tsx` wrapping `<input type="checkbox">` and a `<label>`.
   - Forward refs, apply `aria-checked`, and style custom checkmark via CSS Modules consuming tokens.
3. **Compose a Form:**
   - In `App.tsx`, render a simple login form: `<TextInput label="Username" …/>`, `<TextInput label="Password" type="password" …/>`, `<Checkbox label="Remember me" …/>`, and a `<Button>` to submit.
4. **Deliverable:**
   - Source files for `TextInput` and `Checkbox`.
   - A live form in your app demonstrating controlled state, error styling, and accessible labels.

Key Takeaways

- Form controls must forward refs, handle ARIA attributes, and consume design tokens.
- Variant and size props map directly to token-driven styles in CSS Modules.
- Controlled components ensure predictable state management and validation.

Next Steps
Proceed to **Section 3.2**, where we'll explore layout primitives—Grid, Flexbox, and Container components—to arrange your form controls in responsive, accessible layouts.

3.2 Layout Primitives: Grid, Flexbox, and Container

Goal Statement
In this section you'll learn how to create core layout primitives—`<Container>`, `<Flex>`, and `<Grid>`—that leverage CSS Flexbox and CSS Grid, consume your spacing tokens, and enable responsive, accessible page structures.

Key Terms

- **Container**
- **Flexbox**
- **CSS Grid**
- **Responsive Breakpoints**
- **Gap & Alignment**

Practical Outcome
By the end, you'll implement three layout components with props for direction, alignment, column count, and gaps—using tokens for spacing—and use them to build a responsive card grid.

Research & Gather Notes

- **Official Docs & Blogs**
  - MDN: "Basic concepts of Flexbox" and "CSS Grid Layout".

  - CSS-Tricks: "A Complete Guide to Flexbox" and "A Complete Guide to Grid".
- **Community Examples**
  - GitHub: Chakra UI's `Flex` and `Grid` primitives.
  - GitHub: Tailwind's `container` utility and grid classes.
- **Your Own Experience**
  - Found that abstracting gap and alignment props simplifies repetitive style.
  - Learned to default `<Container>` to max-width breakpoints for consistent layouts.

Building layouts with raw CSS each time leads to inconsistency and repetition. By encapsulating Flexbox and Grid logic into `<Flex>`, `<Grid>`, and `<Container>` components, you provide a declarative, token-driven API for arranging child elements. Layout primitives let designers and developers compose complex UIs—like responsive card galleries or centered hero sections—without writing new CSS.

Our `<Container>` will center content and enforce max-width breakpoints. `<Flex>` exposes props for `direction`, `justify`, `align`, and `gap`, mapping to CSS Flexbox properties. `<Grid>` accepts `columns`, `rowGap`, and `columnGap` props for CSS Grid layouts. All gap and breakpoint values pull from your `tokens.spacing` and a `breakpoints` definition, ensuring consistency across screens.

Concept Breakdown

1. **Container**
   - Centers content horizontally, applies padding via spacing tokens, and constrains to max-width breakpoints (e.g., `640px`, `1024px`).
2. **Flexbox**
   - `display: flex`; `flex-direction`, `justify-content`, `align-items`, and `gap` props control layout.
3. **CSS Grid**
   - `display: grid`; `grid-template-columns` and gap props manage multi-column layouts.
4. **Responsive Breakpoints**
   - Use CSS media queries or container queries to adjust `columns` or `direction` at different viewport widths.
5. **Gap & Alignment**

- Gaps come from `tokens.spacing`; alignment values map to `flex-start`, `center`, `space-between`, etc.

Code Walkthrough

```
// src/components/atoms/Layout/Container.tsx
import React, { PropsWithChildren } from 'react';
import styles from './Container.module.css';
import { tokens } from '../../../styles/tokens';

export function Container({ children }:
PropsWithChildren<{}>) {
  return <div className={styles.container}>{children}</div>;
}
/* src/components/atoms/Layout/Container.module.css */
.container {
  width: 100%;
  margin: 0 auto;
  padding: 0 var(--spacing-2);
  max-width: 1024px;
}
// src/components/atoms/Layout/Flex.tsx
import React, { PropsWithChildren } from 'react';
import styles from './Flex.module.css';
import clsx from 'clsx';

export type FlexDirection = 'row' | 'column';
export type Justify = 'start' | 'center' | 'between' | 'end';
export type Align   = 'start' | 'center' | 'end';

export interface FlexProps extends PropsWithChildren<{}> {
  direction?: FlexDirection;
  justify?: Justify;
  align?: Align;
  gap?: keyof typeof tokens.spacing;
}

export function Flex({
  direction = 'row',
  justify = 'start',
  align = 'start',
  gap = 2,
  children,
}: FlexProps) {
  const classNames = clsx(
    styles.flex,
    styles[`dir-${direction}`],
    styles[`justify-${justify}`],
    styles[`align-${align}`],
    styles[`gap-${gap}`]
```

```
  );
  return <div className={classNames}>{children}</div>;
}
/* src/components/atoms/Layout/Flex.module.css */
.flex { display: flex; }
.dir-row { flex-direction: row; }
.dir-column { flex-direction: column; }
.justify-start { justify-content: flex-start; }
.justify-center { justify-content: center; }
.justify-between { justify-content: space-between; }
.justify-end { justify-content: flex-end; }
.align-start { align-items: flex-start; }
.align-center { align-items: center; }
.align-end { align-items: flex-end; }
/* Token-based gap utilities */
.gap-0 { gap: var(--spacing-0); }
.gap-1 { gap: var(--spacing-1); }
.gap-2 { gap: var(--spacing-2); }
/* etc. */
// src/components/atoms/Layout/Grid.tsx
import React, { PropsWithChildren } from 'react';
import styles from './Grid.module.css';
import clsx from 'clsx';

export interface GridProps extends PropsWithChildren<{}> {
  columns?: number;
  gap?: keyof typeof tokens.spacing;
}

export function Grid({ columns = 3, gap = 2, children }:
GridProps) {
  const classNames = clsx(styles.grid, styles[`cols-
${columns}`], styles[`gap-${gap}`]);
  return <div className={classNames}>{children}</div>;
}
/* src/components/atoms/Layout/Grid.module.css */
.grid { display: grid; }
.cols-1 { grid-template-columns: repeat(1, 1fr); }
.cols-2 { grid-template-columns: repeat(2, 1fr); }
.cols-3 { grid-template-columns: repeat(3, 1fr); }
/* gap utilities as above */
```

- **What it does:**
    - Provides declarative props for layout logic, mapping to CSS modules that consume tokens.
- **Why this approach:**
    - **Reusability:** One component covers many layout scenarios.
    - **Consistency:** Gap and breakpoint values always come from your token set.

Common Pitfalls

1. **Hard-Coded Column Counts**
   - Using fixed numbers without responsive adjustments.
   - **Fix:** Extend `<Grid>` to accept breakpoints or use CSS media queries in styles.
2. **Neglecting Gaps**
   - Overlooking `gap` leads to inconsistent spacing.
   - **Fix:** Always include a `gap` prop, defaulting to your base spacing token.
3. **Misaligned Children**
   - Forgetting `align-items` causes uneven layouts.
   - **Fix:** Provide sensible defaults (`align="start"`, `justify="start"`) and allow overrides.

```
Grid Layout Example (3 columns, gap-2)
┌────────────────────────────────────┐
│ <Grid columns=3 gap=2>             │
│  ┌─────┐ ┌─────┐ ┌─────┐           │
│  │Card1│ │Card2│ │Card3│           │
│  └─────┘ └─────┘ └─────┘           │
└────────────────────────────────────┘
Flex Layout Example (column, center)
┌────────────────────────────────────┐
│ <Flex direction="column"           │
│       align="center" gap=1>        │
│  ┌─────┐                           │
│  │Logo │                           │
│  └─────┘                           │
│  ┌─┐ ┌─┐                           │
│  │Btn Btn│                         │
│  └─┘ └─┘                           │
└────────────────────────────────────┘
```

Hands-On Exercise

Objective: Build a responsive card gallery using your layout primitives.

1. **Create Cards:**
   - Implement a simple `<Card>` component with title and image placeholders.
2. **Compose Grid:**
   - Use `<Grid columns={4} gap={3}>` to layout eight `<Card>` instances.

    - Verify even spacing and layout.
3. **Wrap in Container:**
    - Place your `<Grid>` inside `<Container>` to center and pad on larger viewports.
4. **Make Responsive:**
    - Add a media query so `columns` drops to 2 on small screens (or extend `<Grid>` to accept a `smColumns` prop).
5. **Deliverable:**
    - Source for `Container`, `Flex`, `Grid`, `Card`.
    - Screenshot of desktop (4 columns) and mobile (2 columns) layouts.

Key Takeaways

- Layout primitives abstract Flexbox and Grid into reusable, token-driven components.
- `Container` centers and constrains content; `Flex` manages one-dimensional layouts; `Grid` handles multi-column structures.
- Responsive adjustments and gap props ensure consistent spacing across viewports.

Next Steps
Proceed to **Section 3.3**, where we'll examine atomic vs. composite component patterns to organize and compose more complex UI elements.

3.3 Atomic Components vs. Composite Patterns

Goal Statement
In this section you'll learn to distinguish between **atomic components**—the smallest, single-responsibility UI pieces—and **composite patterns**, which combine atoms into richer, domain-specific UI constructs, enabling both fine-grained reuse and higher-level composition.

Key Terms

- **Atomic Components**
- **Composite Patterns**
- **Single Responsibility**
- **Props-Driven Composition**
- **Abstraction Layers**

Practical Outcome
By the end, you'll be able to categorize existing components as atoms or composites, refactor a composite into its atomic parts, and build a new composite component by composing multiple atoms.

Research & Gather Notes

- **Official Docs & Blogs**
  - Brad Frost's Atomic Design methodology (atoms → molecules → organisms).
  - React docs on "Component Composition" patterns.
- **Community Examples**
  - GitHub: Storybook's "ButtonGroup" example—composing multiple `<Button>` atoms.
  - GitHub: Chakra UI's compound components (e.g., `<Accordion>`, `<Tabs>`).
- **Your Own Experience**
  - I found that moving logic (like open/close state) into a composite component keeps atomic components dumb and easy to test.
  - Learned to pass render-props or child functions for maximum flexibility in composites.

In a design system, **atomic components** are your building blocks—buttons, inputs, icons—each with a single purpose and minimal configuration. **Composite patterns** combine two or more atoms (and possibly other composites) into richer UI constructs like `<FormField>`, `<Modal>`, or `<CardList>`. Thoughtful separation keeps atoms simple and testable, while composites encapsulate behavior and layout specific to a domain or use case.

Atomic components should never know about the application's business logic; they only accept props for style and basic behavior. Composites, on the other hand, may manage state, orchestrate multiple atoms, and enforce consistency across a group of elements (for example, ensuring `<ToggleGroup>` only allows one active item). This layered approach supports both granular reuse and high-level consistency.

Concept Breakdown

1. **Atomic Components**
    - Minimal API (e.g., `<Button>`, `<Icon>`, `<Avatar>`).
    - Stateless or manage only their own local UI state.
    - Serve as inputs to composites.
2. **Composite Patterns**
    - Encapsulate logic: may handle state, context, or event coordination.
    - Combine multiple atoms (and possibly other composites) to form a functional unit.
    - Expose a declarative API (props, render-props, or children as function).
3. **Single Responsibility**
    - Atoms focus solely on rendering.
    - Composites focus on behavior and composition.
4. **Props-Driven Composition**
    - Composites accept props that determine which atoms to render and how.
    - Enables flexibility without leaking internal implementation.
5. **Abstraction Layers**
    - Organize your system into layers: tokens → atoms → composites → pages.
    - Each layer builds on the previous one.

Code Walkthrough

```
// Atom: Button.tsx
export function Button({ children, ...rest }: ButtonProps) {
  return <button {...rest}>{children}</button>;
}

// Composite: ButtonGroup.tsx
import { Button } from './Button';

export interface ButtonGroupProps {
  options: { label: string; onClick: () => void }[];
}

export function ButtonGroup({ options }: ButtonGroupProps) {
  return (
    <div role="group" aria-label="Button group">
      {options.map((opt, i) => (
        <Button key={i} onClick={opt.onClick}>
          {opt.label}
```

```
            </Button>
        ))}
      </div>
  );
}
```

- **What it does:**
  - `<Button>` is a pure atomic component.
  - `<ButtonGroup>` is a composite that orchestrates multiple buttons and groups them for accessibility.
- **Why this approach:**
  - **Testability:** Test `<Button>` in isolation; test `<ButtonGroup>` for mapping logic.
  - **Reusability:** `<Button>` can be used anywhere; `<ButtonGroup>` provides a ready-made pattern.

Common Pitfalls

1. **Over-Composing**
   - Turning atoms into composites when not needed leads to unnecessary complexity.
   - **Fix:** Only create composites when a pattern recurs or when logic coordination is required.
2. **Leaking Logic into Atoms**
   - Embedding state or business rules in atoms reduces their reuse.
   - **Fix:** Keep atoms dumb; lift logic into composite components or hooks.
3. **Tight Coupling**
   - Composites that rely on specific atom internals break when atom APIs change.
   - **Fix:** Use public atom props and avoid importing internal styles or classes.

```
Atomic → Composite Hierarchy

Atoms:              Composites:
┌──────────┐        ┌────────────────────┐
│Button    │------▶│ ButtonGroup        │
└──────────┘        └────────────────────┘

┌──────────┐        ┌────────────────────┐
│Avatar    │------▶│ ProfileCard        │
└──────────┘        │  (Avatar +         │
                    │   Name + Bio)      │
```

Hands-On Exercise

Objective: Refactor and extend your atoms into a new composite.

1. **Identify Atoms:**
   - Ensure you have `<Button>`, `<Avatar>`, and `<Name>` atoms implemented.
2. **Build Composite `<ProfileCard>`:**
   - Accept props `{ avatarUrl, name, onAction }`.
   - Render `<Avatar src={avatarUrl} />`, `<Name>{name}</Name>`, and a `<Button>` that invokes `onAction`.
3. **Expose Flexibility:**
   - Allow a `footer` render-prop so consumers can inject additional controls.
4. **Deliverable:**
   - `ProfileCard.tsx` source and a Storybook story showing default and custom footer usage.

Key Takeaways

- **Atoms** are minimal, single-responsibility components.
- **Composites** orchestrate atoms for richer UI patterns and logic.
- Maintain a clear separation: atoms for presentation, composites for behavior.

Next Steps
Proceed to **Section 3.4**, where we'll dive into accessibility considerations—ensuring your components comply with ARIA roles, keyboard navigation, and screen-reader compatibility.

3.4 Accessibility Considerations and ARIA Best Practices

Goal Statement
In this section you'll learn how to make your React components accessible by following ARIA best practices, semantic HTML usage, and keyboard navigation patterns—ensuring every user, including those relying on assistive technologies, can interact with your UI.

Key Terms

- **Semantic HTML**
- **ARIA Roles & Attributes**
- **Keyboard Focus Management**
- **Screen Reader Announcements**
- **Contrast Ratio**

Practical Outcome
By the end, you'll be able to audit a component for accessibility issues, apply appropriate ARIA attributes, enable complete keyboard interaction, and verify your work using browser devtools and screen-reader testing.

Research & Gather Notes

- **Official Docs & Blogs**
  - W3C's ARIA Authoring Practices (e.g. button, form, modal patterns).
  - MDN Accessibility guide on semantic HTML.
- **Community Examples**
  - GitHub: Reach UI's accessible components (Dialog, Tabs).
  - GitHub: a11yproject's checklist and utilities.
- **Your Own Experience**
  - Found that missing `aria-label` on icon-only buttons left screen-reader users guessing.
  - Learned that `tabIndex` mismanagement can trap keyboard users.

Accessibility is not an afterthought—it's foundational. By using **semantic HTML** (e.g., `<button>`, `<form>`, `<header>`) and augmenting with ARIA only when necessary, you ensure your components convey the right meaning to assistive technology. Beyond markup, proper **keyboard focus management** and clear **screen-reader announcements** guarantee that users who navigate by keyboard or screen reader experience a fluid, understandable interface.

We'll apply these principles to our core components—buttons, inputs, modals—showing how to add ARIA roles (`role="dialog"`), state attributes (`aria-expanded`, `aria-invalid`), and manage `tabIndex`. We'll also cover color contrast, ensuring your token-driven palettes meet WCAG 2.1 AA standards. Finally, we'll demonstrate a simple unit test using `@testing-library/react` to assert accessible properties.

Concept Breakdown

1. **Semantic HTML**
    - Use native elements (`<button>`, `<a>`, `<input>`) before resorting to ARIA roles.
2. **ARIA Roles & Attributes**
    - `role="alert"`, `aria-live="polite"` for announcements.
    - `aria-labelledby` & `aria-describedby` to link labels.
3. **Keyboard Focus Management**
    - `tabIndex={0}` on custom elements; `tabIndex={-1}` to remove from tab order.
    - Manage focus traps in modals.
4. **Screen Reader Announcements**
    - Use live regions (`aria-live`) for dynamic content updates.
5. **Contrast Ratio**
    - Ensure text/background contrast $\geq$ 4.5:1 for normal text, per WCAG AA.

Code Walkthrough

```
// Accessible Button with aria-label for icon-only usage
import React, { forwardRef } from 'react';
import styles from './IconButton.module.css';

interface IconButtonProps extends
React.ButtonHTMLAttributes<HTMLButtonElement> {
  icon: React.ReactNode;
```

```
  label: string;  // Screen-reader text
}

export const IconButton = forwardRef<HTMLButtonElement,
IconButtonProps>(
  ({ icon, label, ...rest }, ref) => (
    <button
      ref={ref}
      className={styles.iconButton}
      aria-label={label}    // Provides accessible name
      {...rest}
    >
      {icon}
    </button>
  )
);
// Form input with aria-invalid and aria-describedby
export function TextInput({
  id,
  label,
  error,
  ...rest
}: {
  id: string;
  label: string;
  error?: string;
} & React.InputHTMLAttributes<HTMLInputElement>) {
  return (
    <div>
      <label htmlFor={id}>{label}</label>
      <input
        id={id}
        aria-invalid={!!error}
        aria-describedby={error ? `${id}-error` : undefined}
        {...rest}
      />
      {error && (
        <span id={`${id}-error`} role="alert">
          {error}
        </span>
      )}
    </div>
  );
}
// Simple Dialog with focus trap (pseudo-code)
export function Modal({ isOpen, onClose, children }) {
  // manage focus on open/close...
  return isOpen ? (
    <div role="dialog" aria-modal="true" className="modal">
      <button onClick={onClose} aria-label="Close
modal">×</button>
```

```
      {children}
    </div>
  ) : null;
}
```

- **What it does:**
  - Provides accessible naming, state, and keyboard support.
- **Why this approach:**
  - Native and ARIA attributes communicate meaning to assistive tech.
  - Focus management prevents keyboard users from escaping modals unintentionally.

Common Pitfalls

1. **Overusing ARIA**
   - Applying `role="button"` on a `<div>` instead of using `<button>`.
   - **Fix:** Prefer semantic elements; use ARIA only when no native option exists.
2. **Missing Keyboard Support**
   - Custom controls without `onKeyDown` handlers for Enter/Space.
   - **Fix:** Implement `onKeyDown` to mirror click behavior (e.g., `if (e.key==='Enter') onClick()`).
3. **Insufficient Contrast**
   - Token-driven colors sometimes fall below 4.5:1 ratio.
   - **Fix:** Run your palette through tools like axe or Contrast Checker and adjust tokens.

```
Focus Order & ARIA Linkage

[ Tab ] -> <label htmlFor="email">Email</label>
[ Tab ] -> <input id="email" aria-describedby="email-error"/>
         [if error] -> <span role="alert" id="email-
error">Invalid email</span>
[ Tab ] -> <button aria-label="Close">×</button>
```

Hands-On Exercise

Objective: Audit and enhance an existing form for complete accessibility.

1. **Audit:**
   - Run `npm install @axe-core/react` and integrate in your app.
   - Use devtools to identify violations in a sample form.
2. **Enhance:**
   - Replace any <div> used as a button with <button>.
   - Add `aria-label` to icon-only buttons.
   - Implement `aria-invalid`, `aria-describedby`, and proper focus order.
3. **Validate:**
   - Confirm no violations in browser console.
   - Test keyboard-only navigation: tab through all interactive elements.
4. **Deliverable:**
   - A before/after report of axe results.
   - Updated component code demonstrating fixes.

Key Takeaways

- **Semantic HTML** plus **ARIA** ensures assistive-technology compatibility.
- Proper **focus management** and **keyboard handlers** are essential.
- Always verify color **contrast** and run automated accessibility audits.

Next Steps
Proceed to **Section 3.5**, where we'll summarize this chapter's learnings and set up exercises to reinforce component building knowledge before moving on to theming.

Component Lifecycle Diagram

```
Component Lifecycle ASCII Diagram

┌──────────────────────────────┐
│  constructor(props)          │
└──────────────────────────────┘
                │
                ▼
┌──────────────────────────────┐
│   render()                   │
```

```
└──────────────────────────────────┘
                │
                ▼
┌──────────────────────────────────┐
│   componentDidMount()            │
└──────────────────────────────────┘
                │
          ┌─────▼─────┐
          │  Update   │
          │ (props/   │
          │  state)   │
          └───────────┘
                │
                ▼
┌──────────────────────────────────┐
│ componentDidUpdate(prev)         │
└──────────────────────────────────┘
                │
                ▼
┌──────────────────────────────────┐
│ componentWillUnmount()           │
└──────────────────────────────────┘
```

3.5 End-of-Chapter Summary & Key Takeaways

1. **Reusable, Accessible Form Controls**
   - Custom `<Button>`, `<TextInput>`, and `<Checkbox>` components consume design tokens, forward refs, and include proper ARIA attributes to ensure consistency and accessibility.
2. **Declarative Layout Primitives**
   - `<Container>`, `<Flex>`, and `<Grid>` abstract common Flexbox and Grid patterns, expose props for direction, alignment, gaps, and rely on spacing tokens for a cohesive layout API.
3. **Atomic vs. Composite Components**
   - **Atoms** (e.g. `<Button>`, `<Avatar>`) are minimal, single-responsibility pieces; **Composites** (e.g. `<ButtonGroup>`, `<ProfileCard>`) orchestrate multiple atoms and encapsulate behavior or patterns.
4. **Accessibility Best Practices**
   - Semantic HTML, ARIA roles/attributes, keyboard focus management, and sufficient color contrast are essential to make components usable by all users and pass automated audits.
5. **Consistent Structure & Patterns**

- Each component follows the same lifecycle: props-driven styling, token consumption, ref forwarding, and modular CSS or styling strategy—ensuring predictability across your design system.

3.6 Hands-On Exercises

Exercise 1: Form Controls Playground

- **Objective:** Solidify your understanding of `<Button>`, `<TextInput>`, and `<Checkbox>` by building a dynamic form.
- **Steps:**
    1. Create a new `FormDemo.tsx` component.
    2. Import your `<TextInput>` and `<Checkbox>`.
    3. Build a "Contact Us" form with fields: Name (`<TextInput>`), Email (`<TextInput>`), Subscribe to newsletter (`<Checkbox>`), and a Submit `<Button>`.
    4. Manage form state with React's `useState`, handling `onChange` and `onSubmit`.
    5. Display validation errors under each input using `aria-invalid` and `aria-describedby`.
- **Deliverable:**
    - A working form component that prevents submission if required fields are empty, highlights errors with red tokens, and logs valid form data to the console.

Exercise 2: Responsive Layout Composition

- **Objective:** Use `<Container>`, `<Flex>`, and `<Grid>` to arrange your form within a responsive page.
- **Steps:**
    1. Wrap your `FormDemo` in `<Container>` to center and pad it.
    2. Above the form, place a centered header using `<Flex direction="column" align="center" gap={2}>` containing a `<h1>` and a subtitle `<p>`.
    3. Below the form, create a `<Grid columns={2} gap={3}>` showcasing two informational cards (reuse your `<Card>` composite from earlier exercises).
    4. Add a media query or conditional prop so that on screens narrower than 600px, the grid drops to one column.

- **Deliverable:**
    - A full-page layout that adapts from two columns on desktop to one column on mobile, demonstrating correct token-driven spacing and alignment.

Exercise 3: Composite Accessibility Audit

- **Objective:** Verify and enhance the accessibility of your composed form and layout.
- **Steps:**
    1. Install and configure `@axe-core/react` in your app.
    2. Navigate through your form using only the keyboard; ensure tab order follows logical flow and focus styles are visible.
    3. Use the browser console to identify any axe violations.
    4. Fix any missing `aria-label`, `aria-describedby`, or focus management issues.
- **Deliverable:**
    - A brief report listing the initial violations, the changes you made, and confirmation of zero violations after fixes. Include screenshots of the form with focus highlights.

These exercises will reinforce your mastery of core components, layout primitives, and accessibility practices—ensuring you're ready to move on to advanced patterns in the next section.

3.7 Next Steps: Applying Accessibility Tests

Goal Statement
In this section you'll learn how to integrate automated accessibility testing into your React development workflow—using tools like `@axe-core/react` and CI–so that every component change is validated against common a11y rules before shipping.

Key Terms

- **Automated A11y Testing**
- **`@axe-core/react`**
- **CI Integration**
- **Violation Reporting**

- **Regression Prevention**

Practical Outcome
By the end, you'll have a working setup that runs accessibility audits in development and Continuous Integration, surfaces violations in the console or pull-request, and blocks merges on new a11y regressions.

Research & Gather Notes

- **Official Docs & Blogs**
  - `@axe-core/react` documentation and examples.
  - GitHub Actions marketplace for a11y checkers (e.g., `pa11y`).
- **Community Examples**
  - GitHub: Microsoft's Fluent UI CI pipeline with axe tests.
  - GitHub: Storybook addon `storybook-addon-a11y`.
- **Your Own Experience**
  - Found that running axe in Storybook catches violations before code lands in the app.
  - Learned to fail CI builds on new violations to enforce team-wide accessibility standards.

Manual accessibility checks catch many issues, but automated tests ensure ongoing compliance. By wiring up `@axe-core/react` in development and adding an axe-based step in your CI pipeline, you create a safety net: every time code is pushed, axe scans your rendered components and reports violations. Teams catching problems early avoid costly remediation later and foster an a11y-first culture.

We'll start by embedding axe in your React app so that violations log in the browser console during development. Then we'll add a Storybook addon to surface issues in your component library. Finally, we'll configure a GitHub Actions workflow that runs axe against a headless browser snapshot of your Storybook and fails on new a11y errors.

Concept Breakdown

1. **`@axe-core/react`**

    - A runtime integration that scans your mounted React tree and logs violations.
2. **Storybook A11y Addon**
    - Displays a11y error panels within Storybook's UI for each story.
3. **CI Workflow**
    - Automates a11y testing on every PR using headless Chrome and axe CLI or `pa11y`.
4. **Violation Reporting**
    - Violations are output as console warnings, Storybook panels, or CI annotations.
5. **Regression Prevention**
    - Failing tests on new violations enforces no–regression policies.

Code Walkthrough

```
// src/setupA11y.tsx
import React from 'react';
import ReactDOM from 'react-dom';
import App from './App';

// Integrate axe in development only
if (process.env.NODE_ENV !== 'production') {
  const axe = require('@axe-core/react');
  axe(React, ReactDOM, 1000);
}

ReactDOM.render(<App />, document.getElementById('root'));
// .storybook/main.js
module.exports = {
  addons: [
    '@storybook/addon-a11y',
    // other addons...
  ],
};
# .github/workflows/a11y.yml
name: Accessibility Test

on: [pull_request]

jobs:
  axe:
    runs-on: ubuntu-latest
    steps:
      - uses: actions/checkout@v3
      - name: Install dependencies
```

```
    run: npm ci
  - name: Build Storybook
    run: npm run build-storybook
  - name: Run Pa11y
    run: npx pa11y-ci --config pa11yci.json
```

- **What it does:**
  - **Dev:** Logs a11y violations in console.
  - **Storybook:** Shows violations per story.
  - **CI:** Fails build on any new violations.
- **Why this approach:**
  - **Early detection:** Catches issues before manual review.
  - **Team enforcement:** Automated pipelines maintain standards.

Common Pitfalls

1. **Performance Overhead**
   - Running axe on every render can slow dev experience.
   - **Fix:** Throttle axe calls (e.g., via the 1000 ms timeout above) or conditionally disable.
2. **False Positives**
   - axe may flag issues in third-party components.
   - **Fix:** Use axe rules configuration to disable or ignore acceptable cases.
3. **Ignoring CI Failures**
   - Teams sometimes override failing checks, defeating the policy.
   - **Fix:** Enforce branch protection rules that disallow merging on a11y failures.

```
Automated A11y Testing Flow

┌─────────────────┐      ┌──────────────┐      ┌──────────────┐
│ Dev Environment │─axe─►Console Logs  │      │ Pull Request │
└─────────────────┘      └──────────────┘      └──────────────┘
        │                       │                      │
        │    Storybook Axe      │     CI A11y Job      │
        └──────────►📖──────────┘     └──pa11y-ci──────┘
```

Hands-On Exercise

Objective: Enable and verify automated accessibility testing in your project.

1. **Dev Integration:**
   - Add `src/setupA11y.tsx` and import it before your root render.
2. **Storybook Addon:**
   - Install `@storybook/addon-a11y` and rebuild Storybook.
   - Open a story and observe the "Accessibility" panel.
3. **CI Job:**
   - Create `.github/workflows/a11y.yml` as above.
   - Commit and open a PR—confirm the a11y job runs and passes.
4. **Deliverable:**
   - Screenshots of console logs, Storybook a11y panel, and a passing CI job.

Key Takeaways

- Integrating `@axe-core/react` surfaces accessibility issues during development.
- Storybook's a11y addon provides in-UI feedback per component.
- CI-level tests prevent regressions and enforce team standards automatically.

Next Steps
Proceed to **Chapter 4**—where we'll dive into theming and variant patterns, using your tested, accessible components as the foundation for light/dark modes and custom brand themes.

Chapter 4: Theming and Variants

4.1 Light, Dark, and Custom Themes with CSS Variables

Goal Statement
In this section you'll learn how to define and switch between light, dark, and arbitrary custom themes by leveraging CSS custom properties (variables) — creating a flexible theming system that updates in real time without touching component logic.

Key Terms

- **CSS Custom Properties**
- **Theming CSS Class**
- **Fallback Values**
- **Theme Override**
- **Dynamic Updates**

Practical Outcome
By the end, you'll be able to author multiple theme token files, apply them via a single root-level CSS class, and switch themes at runtime so your entire design system adapts instantly.

Research & Gather Notes

- **Official Docs & Blogs**
    - MDN: "Using CSS custom properties (CSS variables)."
    - CSS-Tricks: "Dark Mode with CSS Variables" guide.
- **Community Examples**
    - GitHub: Tailwind's dark-mode strategy toggling `class="dark"`.
    - GitHub: Chakra UI's theme overrides using CSS variables.
- **Your Own Experience**
    - Learned that grouping all `--color-*` variables into separate `.light` and `.dark` files prevents staleness.
    - Noted that adding a fallback to `var(--color-primary, #0055FF)` guards against missing definitions.

A robust design system accommodates multiple visual themes—commonly light and dark, but often tailored brand skins as well. By defining your color and spacing tokens as CSS custom properties under different root classes (e.g., `.theme-light`, `.theme-dark`, `.theme-acme`), you separate style data from component logic. Toggling a theme then reduces to swapping one class on `<html>` or `<body>`, instantly updating all components that reference these variables.

We'll begin by refactoring our single `:root` token file into multiple theme-specific CSS files. Each defines the same set of variables but with different values. Next, we'll demonstrate how to apply these classes at runtime (e.g., via a `ThemeProvider`). Finally, we'll add support for an arbitrary "custom" theme—loading user-provided values dynamically into CSS variables.

Concept Breakdown

1. **CSS Custom Properties**
   - Variables declared with `--name` on a selector (`:root`, `.theme-light`) and consumed via `var(--name)`.
2. **Theming CSS Class**
   - A class selector (e.g. `.theme-dark`) that scopes variable values to that theme.
3. **Fallback Values**
   - `var(--color-primary, #0055FF)` ensures a default if the variable isn't defined for a theme.
4. **Theme Override**
   - Later theme classes override earlier ones via CSS specificity or order.
5. **Dynamic Updates**
   - Changing the root element's class name triggers CSS "repaint" without JS-heavy re-renders.

Code Walkthrough

```
/* src/styles/tokens.light.css */
:root.theme-light {
  --color-primary: #0055FF;
  --color-background: #FFFFFF;
  --color-text: #333333;
  --spacing-base: 16px;
}
```

```
/* src/styles/tokens.dark.css */
:root.theme-dark {
  --color-primary: #66B2FF;
  --color-background: #1E1E1E;
  --color-text: #EEEEEE;
  --spacing-base: 16px;
}

/* src/styles/tokens.custom.css */
/* User-supplied overrides (loaded dynamically) */
:root.theme-custom {
  --color-primary: var(--custom-color-primary, #FF00AA);
  --color-background: var(--custom-color-background,
#F0F0F0);
  --color-text: var(--custom-color-text, #222222);
  --spacing-base: var(--custom-spacing-base, 16px);
}
// ThemeProvider.tsx (excerpt)
useEffect(() => {
  const root = document.documentElement;
  root.classList.remove('theme-light', 'theme-dark', 'theme-
custom');
  root.classList.add(`theme-${theme}`); // e.g. 'theme-dark'

  if (theme === 'custom' && customVars) {
    Object.entries(customVars).forEach(([key, value]) => {
      root.style.setProperty(`--${key}`, value);
    });
  }
}, [theme, customVars]);
```

- **What it does:**
    - Defines each theme's variables under a dedicated class.
    - Toggles the class on `<html>` to apply a new theme.
    - For `custom`, injects user values into CSS properties directly.
- **Why this approach:**
    - **Separation of concerns:** Themes live in CSS, components only read variables.
    - **Performance:** Only one class switch; browsers optimize repaint.
    - **Flexibility:** Supports pre-defined and user-generated themes.

Common Pitfalls

1. **Missing Fallbacks**
    - Components break if a variable is absent in a theme.

   - **Fix:** Always use `var(--token, fallback)` or ensure every theme file covers all variables.
2. **Incorrect Class Specificity**
   - Ordering `.theme-light` after `.theme-dark` can prevent overrides.
   - **Fix:** Load CSS in logical order or increase specificity (e.g., `:root.theme-dark`).
3. **Style Leakage**
   - Inline setting of CSS variables may not clean up when theme changes.
   - **Fix:** Remove or reset custom properties when switching away from custom theme.

```
Theme Switch State Machine
┌─────────────────┐        toggle        ┌─────────────────┐
│ theme-light     │ ───────────────────► │ theme-dark      │
└─────────────────┘                      └─────────────────┘
        ▲                                        │
        │              toggle                    │
        └────────────────────────────────────────┘
              │
              ▼
      ┌─────────────────┐
      │ theme-custom    │
      │ (user values)   │
      └─────────────────┘
```

Hands-On Exercise

Objective: Configure and test multiple themes in your app.

1. **Add Theme CSS:**
   - Create `tokens.light.css`, `tokens.dark.css`, and `tokens.custom.css` under `src/styles/`, each defining the core variables.
2. **Extend `ThemeProvider`:**
   - Update the provider to accept `customVars: Record<string,string>` for user themes.
   - Ensure it sets inline CSS properties when `theme === 'custom'`.
3. **Build UI Controls:**
   - Add a `<select>` or toggle buttons in your app header to choose between "Light," "Dark," and "Custom."

    - For “Custom,” present inputs to set `--custom-color-primary` and `--custom-color-background`.
4. **Verify:**
    - Switching themes updates component colors instantly.
    - Custom values persist until theme changes again.
5. **Deliverable:**
    - Updated CSS files, `ThemeProvider.tsx`, and a screenshot or screencast showing theme transitions (including custom values).

Key Takeaways

- Themes are implemented by scoping CSS variables under root classes.
- Toggling a class on `<html>` applies a new theme with minimal JS.
- Custom themes load user-provided values directly into CSS properties.

Next Steps
Proceed to **Section 4.2**, where we'll implement the `<ThemeSwitcher>` component and persistence logic—enabling seamless theme selection and storage across sessions.

4.2 Theme Switcher Implementation in React

Goal Statement
In this section you'll learn how to build a reusable `<ThemeSwitcher>` component—hooked into your `ThemeProvider`—that allows users to toggle between light, dark, and custom themes, persisting their choice across sessions.

Key Terms

- **React Context API**
- **Custom Hook**
- **Local Storage Persistence**
- **Controlled Component**
- **Side Effects**

Practical Outcome
By the end, you'll have a `<ThemeSwitcher>` control that reads and updates the current theme via context, persists the selection in `localStorage`, and reflects the change immediately in the UI.

Research & Gather Notes

- **Official Docs & Blogs**
  - React docs: "Using the Context API" for global state.
  - React docs: "Using the Effect Hook" for side effects like localStorage.
- **Community Examples**
  - GitHub: Chakra UI's ColorModeSwitcher implementation.
  - Blog post: Kent C. Dodds on building custom hooks for theme persistence.
- **Your Own Experience**
  - Persisting UI preferences in `localStorage` on initial render prevents flicker.
  - Extracting logic into a `useTheme` hook simplifies component code.

A seamless theme switcher enhances user experience by remembering their preference and applying it immediately on page load. We'll implement `<ThemeSwitcher>` as a simple select dropdown (or icon button group) that invokes `useTheme()` from our context. Under the hood, we'll read `localStorage` on mount to initialize the theme, update both context state and `localStorage` on change, and ensure that our CSS-class toggling logic in `ThemeProvider` reflects the new value.

Breaking this into a custom hook—`usePersistedTheme()`—lets us encapsulate the side-effect logic and use it across any component, while keeping `<ThemeSwitcher>` purely presentational and declarative.

Concept Breakdown

1. **React Context API**
   - Provides `theme` and `setTheme` throughout the app.

2. **Custom Hook (`usePersistedTheme`)**
   - Reads from `localStorage` on mount; writes to it on theme changes.
3. **Side Effects (`useEffect`)**
   - Syncs context state with `localStorage` and triggers class changes.
4. **Controlled Component**
   - `<select>` value bound to `theme`; `onChange` updates context.
5. **Immediate UI Feedback**
   - Changing the theme value re-renders the UI with new CSS variables.

Code Walkthrough

```
// src/theme/usePersistedTheme.ts
import { useState, useEffect } from 'react';
import { Theme } from './ThemeContext';

const STORAGE_KEY = 'app-theme';

export function usePersistedTheme(): [Theme, (t: Theme) =>
void] {
  const [theme, setTheme] = useState<Theme>('light');

  // On mount, read stored theme
  useEffect(() => {
    const stored = localStorage.getItem(STORAGE_KEY) as Theme
| null;
    if (stored) setTheme(stored);
  }, []);

  // Persist on theme change
  useEffect(() => {
    localStorage.setItem(STORAGE_KEY, theme);
  }, [theme]);

  return [theme, setTheme];
}
// src/theme/ThemeProvider.tsx (excerpt)
import React, { createContext, useContext } from 'react';
import { usePersistedTheme } from './usePersistedTheme';

type ThemeContextValue = {
  theme: Theme;
  setTheme: (t: Theme) => void;
};
const ThemeContext = createContext<ThemeContextValue>({
theme: 'light', setTheme: () => {} });
```

```
export function ThemeProvider({ children }: { children:
React.ReactNode }) {
  const [theme, setTheme] = usePersistedTheme();

  // class toggling logic here...
  // (same as in Section 4.1)

  return (
    <ThemeContext.Provider value={{ theme, setTheme }}>
      {children}
    </ThemeContext.Provider>
  );
}

export const useTheme = () => useContext(ThemeContext);
// src/components/ThemeSwitcher/ThemeSwitcher.tsx
import React from 'react';
import { useTheme } from '../../theme/ThemeProvider';

export function ThemeSwitcher() {
  const { theme, setTheme } = useTheme();

  return (
    <label>
      Theme: 
      <select value={theme} onChange={e =>
setTheme(e.target.value as any)}>
        <option value="light">Light</option>
        <option value="dark">Dark</option>
        <option value="custom">Custom</option>
      </select>
    </label>
  );
}
```

- **What it does:**
    - `usePersistedTheme` initializes and persists the theme in `localStorage`.
    - `ThemeProvider` wraps the app, supplying `theme` and `setTheme`.
    - `<ThemeSwitcher>` renders a controlled select to pick the theme.
- **Why this approach:**
    - **Separation of concerns:** Persistence logic lives in a hook; presentation in a component.
    - **Reusability:** You can swap `<ThemeSwitcher>` for any UI (radio buttons, toggles) without touching logic.

- **Instant feedback:** Changing the select updates CSS variables immediately.

Common Pitfalls

1. **Flicker on First Render**
    - The app may render in default theme before `useEffect` runs.
    - **Fix:** Initialize state from `localStorage` directly in `useState`:
    - `const initial = (localStorage.getItem(STORAGE_KEY) as Theme) || 'light';`
    - `const [theme, setTheme] = useState<Theme>(initial);`
2. **Invalid Stored Values**
    - Corrupted or unsupported values in `localStorage` can break.
    - **Fix:** Validate against allowed themes before setting state.
3. **Overwriting Custom Theme Variables**
    - Switching away from 'custom' may leave old CSS vars in place.
    - **Fix:** In `ThemeProvider`, remove inline styles for custom keys when leaving custom mode.

<ThemeSwitcher> Flow

```
┌───────────────────┐
│ usePersistedTheme │
│ theme, setTheme   │
└───────────────────┘
         │
         ▼
┌───────────────────┐
│ <select value=theme│
│  onChange=setTheme │
└───────────────────┘
         │
         ▼
┌───────────────────┐
│ ThemeContext updates│
│ ThemeProvider effect│
└───────────────────┘
```

Hands-On Exercise

Objective: Build a styled toggle UI for `<ThemeSwitcher>` and handle persistence edge cases.

1. **Custom UI:**
   - Replace the `<select>` with three icon buttons (sun, moon, palette).
   - Highlight the active theme button.
2. **No-Flicker Initialization:**
   - Refactor `usePersistedTheme` to read `localStorage` in the initial state, avoiding a re-render.
3. **Validation:**
   - Guard against invalid `localStorage` entries by defaulting to `'light'` if the stored value isn't one of `['light','dark','custom']`.
4. **Deliverable:**
   - Updated `usePersistedTheme.ts`, a styled `ThemeSwitcher.tsx`, and screenshots or a short gif showing no initial flicker and correct toggle behavior.

Key Takeaways

- Encapsulate theme persistence in a custom hook using `useState` and `useEffect`.
- Build `<ThemeSwitcher>` as a controlled, reusable component separate from logic.
- Avoid UI flicker by initializing state with the stored value and validate inputs.

Next Steps
Proceed to **Section 4.3**, where we'll handle responsive typography and spacing variants—adjusting token-driven scales based on viewport size.

4.3 Handling Responsive Breakpoints and Fluid Typography

Goal Statement
In this section you'll learn how to define and consume responsive breakpoints and implement fluid typography—using CSS variables, media queries, and the `clamp()` function—so your UI scales gracefully across all viewports.

Key Terms

- **Breakpoint**
- **Media Query**
- **Fluid Typography**
- **clamp()**
- **CSS Custom Properties**

Practical Outcome
By the end, you'll be able to author breakpoint variables, apply them in media queries, and create typographic scales that smoothly adjust between a minimum and maximum size using `clamp()`, ensuring legible text on mobile through desktop.

Research & Gather Notes

- **Official Docs & Blogs**
    - MDN: "Using CSS media queries" and "Clamp() CSS function."
    - CSS-Tricks: "Fluid Typography with clamp()" guide.
- **Community Examples**
    - GitHub: Tailwind's responsive design tokens (`sm`, `md`, `lg`).
    - GitHub: CSS-in-JS libraries demonstrating fluid type scaling.
- **Your Own Experience**
    - Discovered that using CSS variables for breakpoints ensures consistency across components.
    - Learned that `clamp()` provides native fluid scaling without JavaScript or complex calculations.

As screen sizes proliferate—from small phones to large desktops—your design system must adapt. **Breakpoints** let you apply different layouts or styles at specified viewport widths. Meanwhile, **fluid typography** ensures text grows and shrinks in proportion, improving readability without abrupt jumps. By defining breakpoints and employing a `clamp()`-based typographic scale, you marry control with flexibility: headings expand on wide screens yet remain readable on mobile.

We'll first declare our breakpoints as CSS custom properties (`--breakpoint-sm`, etc.) and then use them in media queries within our components. Next, we'll build a fluid type scale: defining minimum, preferred, and maximum font sizes for headings and body text using `clamp()`. Finally, we'll combine these techniques to create a `<ResponsiveText>` utility that applies the correct sizing automatically.

Concept Breakdown

1. **Breakpoint**
   - Named viewport widths (e.g., `sm = 640px`, `md = 1024px`) used in media queries.
2. **Media Query**
   - CSS rule (`@media (min-width: var(--breakpoint-md))`) to apply styles at or above a breakpoint.
3. **Fluid Typography**
   - Dynamic font sizing between two thresholds, calculated by `clamp(min, preferred, max)`.
4. **clamp() Function**
   - Native CSS that limits a value between a lower and upper bound: `clamp(1rem, 2vw + 1rem, 1.5rem)`.
5. **CSS Custom Properties**
   - Variables that store breakpoints or scale factors, ensuring consistency.

Code Walkthrough

```
/* src/styles/breakpoints.css */
:root {
  --breakpoint-sm: 640px;
  --breakpoint-md: 1024px;
  --breakpoint-lg: 1280px;
}
/* src/components/atoms/Typography/ResponsiveText.module.css
*/
:root {
  /* Fluid scale for body text */
  --font-body-min: 1rem;          /* 16px */
  --font-body-max: 1.125rem;      /* 18px */
  --font-body-preferred: 2vw;     /* scales with viewport width
*/

  /* Fluid scale for heading */
  --font-heading-min: 2rem;         /* 32px */
  --font-heading-max: 3rem;         /* 48px */
```

```
  --font-heading-preferred: 4vw; /* scales with viewport
width */
}

.responsive-body {
  font-size: clamp(
    var(--font-body-min),
    var(--font-body-preferred) + var(--font-body-min),
    var(--font-body-max)
  );
  line-height: 1.6;
}

.responsive-heading {
  font-size: clamp(
    var(--font-heading-min),
    var(--font-heading-preferred) + var(--font-heading-min),
    var(--font-heading-max)
  );
  line-height: 1.2;
}

/* Example breakpoint override */
@media (min-width: var(--breakpoint-md)) {
  .responsive-heading {
    /* Increase max on larger screens */
    font-size: clamp(
      var(--font-heading-min),
      var(--font-heading-preferred) + var(--font-heading-
min),
      4rem /* richer max at md+ */
    );
  }
}
// src/components/atoms/Typography/ResponsiveText.tsx
import React from 'react';
import clsx from 'clsx';
import styles from './ResponsiveText.module.css';

export type TextVariant = 'body' | 'heading';

export interface ResponsiveTextProps {
  variant?: TextVariant;
  children: React.ReactNode;
}

export function ResponsiveText({ variant = 'body', children
}: ResponsiveTextProps) {
  const className = clsx({
    [styles['responsive-body']]: variant === 'body',
    [styles['responsive-heading']]: variant === 'heading',
```

```
  });
  return <div className={className}>{children}</div>;
}
```

- **What it does:**
  - Breakpoints defined as CSS vars are used in media queries.
  - Fluid font scales use `clamp(min, preferred + min, max)` to interpolate sizes.
  - `<ResponsiveText>` applies the appropriate CSS class per variant.
- **Why this approach:**
  - **Consistency:** All components reference the same breakpoints and scale factors.
  - **Performance:** Native CSS handles resizing; no JavaScript needed.
  - **Readability:** Smooth transitions avoid jarring text size jumps.

Common Pitfalls

1. **Poorly Calibrated Ranges**
   - Mismatched min/max can produce too-small or too-large text.
   - **Fix:** Test across devices and adjust bounds for comfort.
2. **Neglecting Line Height**
   - Fluid font-size without proper line-height can break readability.
   - **Fix:** Pair each fluid scale with a fixed, proportional line-height.
3. **Media Query Overrides**
   - Overriding in media queries may conflict with `clamp()` preferred values.
   - **Fix:** Use media queries sparingly for only necessary adjustments.

```
Fluid Typography Scale

Viewport Width →
┌──────────────────────────────────────────────────┐
│ clamp(min, preferred+min, max)                   │
│ ┌────────────────────────────────────────────┐   │
│ │         fluid curve between min & max      │   │
│ └────────────────────────────────────────────┘   │
└──────────────────────────────────────────────────┘

Breakpoints
```

```
┌──────────────┐   ┌────────────────┐   ┌────────────────┐
│     sm       │   │      md        │   │      lg        │
│ (640px)      │   │ (1024px)       │   │ (1280px)       │
└──────────────┘   └────────────────┘   └────────────────┘
```

Hands-On Exercise

Objective: Implement fluid typography and responsive layout in a real component.

1. **Set Breakpoints:**
   - Define `--breakpoint-sm`, `--breakpoint-md`, `--breakpoint-lg` in your global CSS.
2. **Create Fluid Scale:**
   - Copy the `clamp()` rules for body and heading into a `Typography.module.css`.
3. **Build <ResponsiveText>:**
   - Implement the component as shown and render a sample heading and paragraph.
4. **Test Responsiveness:**
   - Resize the browser from narrow to wide and observe smooth text scaling.
5. **Deliverable:**
   - Screenshot or gif demonstrating fluid sizing for a heading and paragraph across viewport widths (mobile, tablet, desktop).

Key Takeaways

- Breakpoints stored in CSS variables ensure consistent media-query thresholds.
- Fluid typography with `clamp()` provides smooth scaling between defined min and max sizes.
- Combining `clamp()` with media queries yields precise control over text sizing on all devices.

Next Steps

Proceed to **Section 4.4**, where we'll explore **Dynamic Token Overrides with TypeScript Interfaces**—tying together our CSS and TS token management to enable fully type-safe runtime theme adjustments.

4.4 Dynamic Token Overrides with TypeScript Interfaces

Goal Statement
In this section you'll learn how to expose your design tokens through a TypeScript interface so consumers can provide custom overrides at runtime—with full compile-time safety—enabling on-the-fly theming and brand variants.

Key Terms

- **Token Override**
- **TypeScript Interface**
- **`Partial<T>` Utility**
- **Runtime Injection**
- **Default Fallbacks**

Practical Outcome
By the end, you'll define a `ThemeTokens` interface matching your CSS-variable structure, extend your `ThemeProvider` API to accept a `customTokens: Partial<ThemeTokens>`, and merge defaults with overrides so that only valid keys can be supplied.

Research & Gather Notes

- **Official Docs & Blogs**
  - TypeScript handbook: "Utility Types" (`Partial`, `Pick`).
  - MDN: "CSS Custom Properties and JavaScript."
- **Community Examples**
  - GitHub: Chakra UI's `extendTheme` API which types theme overrides.
  - GitHub: Material-UI's `ThemeOptions` interface.
- **Your Own Experience**
  - Learned that using `Partial<T>` combined with deep merging utilities (e.g. `lodash.merge`) enforces override shape while preserving defaults.
  - Discovered that inlining CSS properties via JS needs cleanup logic to avoid stale values.

While root-class theming covers preset light, dark, and custom files, advanced applications often need to let end users or designers tweak individual token values—colors, spacing steps, or typography scales—at runtime. By defining a TypeScript interface that mirrors your token structure, you guarantee that any override object only includes known token keys, and you can merge these overrides against your default tokens before injecting them into CSS custom properties.

Concept Breakdown

1. **Token Override**
   - Supplying a subset of tokens (`{ color: { primary: '#abc123' } }`) to change only what's needed.
2. **TypeScript Interface**
   - `ThemeTokens` captures every token category and key as in your `tokens` object.
3. **`Partial<T>` Utility**
   - Makes every property optional, allowing overrides of just one category or token.
4. **Runtime Injection**
   - Merging default tokens with overrides and calling `root.style.setProperty()` for each.
5. **Default Fallbacks**
   - Unoverridden values remain from the base theme, preventing undefined CSS variables.

Code Walkthrough

```
// src/theme/tokens.ts
export interface ThemeTokens {
  color: {
    primary: string;
    secondary: string;
    success: string;
    text: string;
  };
  spacing: Record<0 | 1 | 2 | 3, string>;
  fontSize: Record<0 | 1 | 2 | 3 | 4, string>;
}

// Default tokens, as before
export const defaultTokens: ThemeTokens = { /* …var()
references… */ } as const;
// src/theme/ThemeProvider.tsx (excerpt)
import merge from 'lodash.merge';
```

```
import { defaultTokens, ThemeTokens } from './tokens';

export type CustomTokens = Partial<{
  [K in keyof ThemeTokens]: Partial<ThemeTokens[K]>
}>;

export function ThemeProvider({ children, customTokens }: {
children: React.ReactNode; customTokens?: CustomTokens }) {
  // Merge default + overrides
  const merged = merge({}, defaultTokens, customTokens ||
{});

  // Inject each CSS variable
  useEffect(() => {
    const root = document.documentElement;
    Object.entries(merged).forEach(([category, values]) => {
      Object.entries(values as
Record<string,string>).forEach(([key, val]) => {
        root.style.setProperty(`--${category}-${key}`, val);
      });
    });
  }, [customTokens]);

  // …rest of provider…
}
```

- **What it does:**
  - Defines `ThemeTokens` to type your token shape.
  - Uses `Partial` mapped type so `customTokens` can omit any category or key.
  - Deep-merges defaults with overrides and updates CSS variables accordingly.
- **Why this approach:**
  - **Type Safety:** Attempts to override non-existent tokens produce compile errors.
  - **Flexibility:** Consumers override only what they need without boilerplate.
  - **Consistency:** Unchanged tokens fall back to defaults automatically.

Common Pitfalls

1. **Incorrect Merge Order**
   - Merging into the defaults object mutates it.
   - **Fix:** Always merge into a fresh object: `merge({}, defaultTokens, customTokens)`.

2. **Stale CSS Variables**
   - Removing a key from `customTokens` doesn't revert its CSS var.
   - **Fix:** On theme change, clean all variables first or reset inline styles before re-injection.
3. **Overly Broad `Partial`**
   - Using `any` instead of Partial<ThemeTokens> loses safety.
   - **Fix:** Declare overrides with precise mapped types as above.

```
Custom Token Override Flow

defaultTokens ──┐
                ▼
           merge() ───▶ mergedTokens
                │
                ▼
   setProperty(--color-primary, merged.color.primary)
   setProperty(--spacing-2, merged.spacing[2])
```

Hands-On Exercise

Objective: Allow users to override your primary color and spacing token at runtime.

1. **Extend Provider:**
   - Add `customTokens` prop to your `ThemeProvider` and implement merging as shown.
2. **Write Interface:**
   - Confirm `ThemeTokens` matches your CSS vars exactly; try overriding an invalid key to see a TypeScript error.
3. **Consume Overrides:**
   - In your app, pass `{ color: { primary: '#e91e63' }, spacing: { 2: '24px' } }` to <ThemeProvider>.
4. **Verify:**
   - Inspect computed CSS variables in the browser; the overridden values should apply and defaults persist.
5. **Deliverable:**
   - Updated `tokens.ts`, `ThemeProvider.tsx`, and a screenshot of the changed styles reflected in your UI.

Key Takeaways

- Use a `ThemeTokens` interface to model your token structure in TypeScript.

- Partial<ThemeTokens> enables safe, granular overrides with compile-time checks.
- Deep-merge defaults with overrides and inject only the resulting CSS variables, preserving fallbacks.

Next Steps
Proceed to **Chapter 5.1**, where we'll set up Storybook for your design system—documenting each component and visualizing both default and custom-token themes in isolation.

Visual Aid: Theme Switch State-Transition Flowchart

```
Theme Switch State-Transition Flowchart

┌─────────────────┐        toggle        ┌─────────────────┐
│ theme-light     │  ──────────────────▶ │ theme-dark      │
└─────────────────┘                      └─────────────────┘
        │                                        │
        │                toggle                  │
        └────────────────────────────────────────┘
             │
             ▼
      ┌─────────────────┐
      │ theme-custom    │
      │ (user values)   │
      └─────────────────┘
```

4.5 End-of-Chapter Summary & Key Takeaways

1. **Multiple Theme Definitions**
    - Themes are authored as separate CSS-variable files scoped under root classes (e.g., .theme-light, .theme-dark, .theme-custom).
    - Each file declares the same token names with different values, ensuring consistency across themes.
2. **Runtime Theme Switching**
    - A single class toggle on <html> or <body> applies a new theme instantly, leveraging browser CSS optimizations.
    - Custom themes can inject user-provided values via inline CSS variables for maximum flexibility.
3. **Persisted Theme State**

- Encapsulating persistence logic in a custom `usePersistedTheme` hook stores the user's choice in `localStorage` and initializes state without UI flicker.
    - The `ThemeProvider` uses Context to supply `theme` and `setTheme` to all components.
4. **Responsive & Fluid Styling**
    - Breakpoints defined as CSS variables (`--breakpoint-sm`, `--breakpoint-md`, etc.) enable consistent media-query thresholds.
    - Fluid typography uses the `clamp()` function with CSS variables to smoothly scale text sizes between defined minimum and maximum values.
5. **Type-Safe Token Overrides**
    - Defining a `ThemeTokens` TypeScript interface and using `Partial<ThemeTokens>` ensures only valid token keys can be overridden.
    - Merging default tokens with overrides before injecting CSS variables preserves fallbacks and prevents runtime errors.

With these theming techniques—scoped CSS variables, Context-driven switching, persisted user preferences, responsive scales, and type-safe overrides—you're equipped to implement robust, flexible, and user-friendly themes in your React design system. Next, we'll set up Storybook in Chapter 5 to document and preview these themes alongside your components.

4.6 Hands-On Exercises

Exercise 1: Scaffold and Apply Theme CSS Files

- **Objective:** Create and verify your light, dark, and custom theme definitions.
- **Steps:**
    1. Under `src/styles/`, create three files: `tokens.light.css`, `tokens.dark.css`, and `tokens.custom.css`, each declaring your core CSS variables (colors, background, text, spacing) under `.theme-light`, `.theme-dark`, and `.theme-custom` selectors.
    2. Import all three in your global stylesheet (e.g. `index.css`) so they're bundled.

3. Manually add and remove the classes on `<html>` (via DevTools) to confirm the variables update.

- **Deliverable:** Screenshots showing your app in light, dark, and custom themes (you can override one or two variables inline for "custom").

Exercise 2: Build and Test the `<ThemeSwitcher>` Component

- **Objective:** Implement the user control for theme toggling with persistence.
- **Steps:**
  1. Create the `usePersistedTheme` hook that initializes state from `localStorage` and writes back on updates (avoid flicker by seeding `useState` from `localStorage`).
  2. Build a `<ThemeSwitcher>` component (e.g. select dropdown or icon buttons) that reads and sets the theme via your `ThemeContext`.
  3. Wrap your app in `ThemeProvider` and render `<ThemeSwitcher>` prominently (e.g. in the header).
  4. Reload the page to verify the selected theme persists and no flash of default occurs.
- **Deliverable:** A short screencast or series of screenshots showing theme selection, persistence across reloads, and correct class on `<html>`.

Exercise 3: Verify Responsive and Fluid Styles Under Each Theme

- **Objective:** Ensure your breakpoints and fluid typography work correctly in all themes.
- **Steps:**
  1. In your token CSS, define breakpoint variables (`--breakpoint-sm`, `--breakpoint-md`, `--breakpoint-lg`).
  2. In a component (e.g. `<ResponsiveText>`), apply fluid `clamp()` rules for body and heading text.
  3. Using DevTools, emulate mobile, tablet, and desktop widths to observe smooth text scaling and any media-query overrides.

4. While switching between light, dark, and custom themes, confirm that typography and layout remain responsive and legible.

- **Deliverable:** A GIF or set of screenshots showing the same text element resizing fluidly at different viewport widths under each theme.

These exercises will solidify your mastery of CSS-variable theming, Context-driven switchers with persistence, and responsive/fluid design under multiple themes—preparing you to document and demo them in Storybook in the next chapter.

4.7 Next Steps: Building Custom Theme Editor

Goal Statement
In this section you'll learn how to build a simple in-app theme editor that lets users tweak token values (colors, spacing) via a UI, preview changes live, and export their custom theme settings.

Key Terms

- **Dynamic Form Controls**
- **Two-Way Binding**
- **Live Preview**
- **JSON Export**
- **Validation**

Practical Outcome
By the end, you'll have a `<ThemeEditor>` component where users can adjust inputs (color pickers, sliders), see the app's CSS variables update in real time, and download a JSON file of their customTokens payload.

Research & Gather Notes

- **Official Docs & Blogs**
  - MDN: "Using the `<input type="color">`" and range sliders.
  - React docs: "Lifting state up" for controlled components.
- **Community Examples**

- GitHub: theme editors in Storybook's "Controls" panel.
- CodeSandbox: live CSS-variable playgrounds.

- **Your Own Experience**
  - Found that debouncing updates prevents excessive reflows.
  - Learned that exporting a JSON blob via a `data:` URL is the simplest download strategy.

A custom theme editor empowers end users to fine-tune your design system without digging into code. By binding form inputs directly to your `ThemeProvider`'s `customTokens`, you can reflect every adjustment immediately in the UI. Then, by serializing the final token object to JSON and offering it as a downloadable file, users can save and share their bespoke themes.

Concept Breakdown

1. **Dynamic Form Controls**
   - Use `<input type="color">` for color tokens and `<input type="range">` for numeric spacing.
2. **Two-Way Binding**
   - Form values update `customTokens` in context; context changes update form values.
3. **Live Preview**
   - As soon as `customTokens` changes, `ThemeProvider` injects new CSS variables and the app repaints.
4. **JSON Export**
   - Convert the `customTokens` object to a JSON string and create a downloadable link with `URL.createObjectURL`.
5. **Validation**
   - Ensure color inputs yield valid hex codes and spacing sliders stay within acceptable ranges.

`<ThemeEditor> Data Flow`

```
┌──────────────────┐        onChange          ┌───────────────┐
│ Color Picker     │ ───────────────────────▶ │ customTokens  │
└──────────────────┘                          └───────────────┘
          │                                          │
          │                                          ▼
          │                                   ┌────────────────┐
          │                                   │ CSS Variables  │
          └─────────────────────────────────▶│ updated via    │
                                              │ ThemeProvider  │
```

Hands-On Exercise

Objective: Build and integrate a `<ThemeEditor>` UI.

1. **Create Controls:**
   - For each color token (e.g. `primary`, `background`), render a color input.
   - For each spacing token, render a range slider bounded by min/max spacing values.
2. **Bind to Context:**
   - Consume `customTokens` and `setCustomTokens` from `useTheme()`.
   - On input change, merge the new value into `customTokens`.
3. **Live Update:**
   - Ensure changes immediately reflect in the app's appearance.
4. **Implement Export:**
   - Add a "Download JSON" button that serializes `customTokens` to a file named `theme.json`.
5. **Deliverable:**
   - Source code for `ThemeEditor.tsx`, screenshots of the editor UI, and a downloaded `theme.json` sample.

Key Takeaways

- A custom theme editor uses controlled inputs bound to `customTokens` for live update.
- Two-way binding and debouncing keep the UI responsive.
- JSON export lets users save and reuse their themes.

Next Steps
Proceed to **Chapter 5**, where we'll configure Storybook to document all components and showcase your default and custom-token themes side by side.

Chapter 5: Documenting with Storybook

5.1 Setting Up Storybook for Your Library

Goal Statement
In this section you'll learn how to integrate Storybook into your React design-system project—configuring it to load your components, apply your global styles and tokens, and serve as an interactive playground and documentation hub.

Key Terms

- **Storybook CLI**
- **Main Configuration (`main.js`)**
- **Preview Configuration (`preview.js`)**
- **Addons**
- **Webpack Aliases**

Practical Outcome
By the end, you'll have a fully functional Storybook instance that displays your components in isolation, applies your design-system's CSS variables and global decorators, and leverages essential addons for controls, documentation, and accessibility.

Research & Gather Notes

- **Official Docs & Blogs**
  - Storybook "Get Started" guide.
  - Storybook "Configuration" documentation (main.js, preview.js).
- **Community Examples**
  - GitHub: Airbnb's `react-dates` Storybook setup.
  - GitHub: Chakra UI's monorepo Storybook config.
- **Your Own Experience**
  - Learned to set up Webpack aliases so `import { Button } from 'components'` works in stories.
  - Found that adding global decorators for theme and tokens ensures stories render with correct styling.

Storybook provides a sandboxed environment for developing, testing, and documenting UI components. Instead of running your entire app, you mount individual components with custom props ("stories") and leverage addons like **Controls** for live prop editing, **Docs** for autogenerated documentation, and **A11y** for accessibility checks. Let's scaffold Storybook, configure it to load your design-system code, and wire in global parameters and decorators so every story uses your CSS variables, theme provider, and token overrides.

Concept Breakdown

1. **Storybook CLI**
   - `npx sb init` boots a basic configuration inside your project, detecting React and installing core addons.
2. **`main.js` Configuration**
   - Defines where stories live (glob patterns), which addons to load, and custom Webpack settings (e.g., aliases to `src/`).
3. **`preview.js` Configuration**
   - Exports parameters (e.g., backgrounds, viewport sizes) and decorators (wrappers) to apply to all stories, such as your `<ThemeProvider>`.
4. **Addons**
   - Plugins that extend Storybook:
     - **@storybook/addon-controls** for live prop editing.
     - **@storybook/addon-docs** for Markdown/MDX docs.
     - **@storybook/addon-a11y** for accessibility insights.
5. **Webpack Aliases**
   - Simplify imports by aliasing `components` or `styles` to absolute paths, matching your app's configuration.

Code Walkthrough

```
# 1. Install Storybook
npx sb init --builder webpack5
// .storybook/main.js
module.exports = {
  stories:
['../src/components/**/*.stories.@(js|jsx|ts|tsx|mdx)'],
  addons: [
    '@storybook/addon-essentials',
    '@storybook/addon-a11y',
  ],
  webpackFinal: async (config) => {
    // Alias 'components' to src/components
    config.resolve.alias = {
```

```
      ...(config.resolve.alias || {}),
      components: path.resolve(__dirname,
'../src/components'),
      styles: path.resolve(__dirname, '../src/styles'),
    };
    return config;
  },
};
// .storybook/preview.js
import React from 'react';
import { ThemeProvider } from '../src/theme/ThemeProvider';
import '../src/styles/index.css'; // global CSS + token
imports

export const decorators = [
  (Story) => (
    <ThemeProvider>
      <div style={{ padding: '20px' }}>
        <Story />
      </div>
    </ThemeProvider>
  ),
];

export const parameters = {
  actions: { argTypesRegex: '^on[A-Z].*' },
  controls: { expanded: true },
  a11y: { element: '#root' },
};
```

- **What it does:**
  - Installs Storybook and essentials.
  - Tells Storybook where your stories live.
  - Adds aliases so imports mimic your application.
  - Wraps every story in `<ThemeProvider>` and global CSS to reflect true design-system styling.
- **Why this approach:**
  - **Isolation:** Components render without app overhead.
  - **Consistency:** Stories use the same tokens, themes, and styles as your app.
  - **Discoverability:** Addons surface props, documentation, and accessibility considerations at a glance.

Common Pitfalls

1. **Misplaced Stories**
   - Story filenames not matching the glob pattern.

- **Fix:** Ensure stories follow `*.stories.tsx` (or MDX) under `src/components/**`.

2. **Missing Global Styles**
   - Stories render unstyled components.
   - **Fix:** Import your main `index.css` or vars file in `preview.js`.
3. **Alias Mismatch**
   - Aliases in Storybook differ from your app, causing import errors.
   - **Fix:** Mirror your app's Webpack/TS aliases in `.storybook/main.js`.

```
Storybook Initialization Flow

npx sb init
    |
    ▼
.storybook/
├── main.js   # stories, addons, webpackFinal
└── preview.js# decorators, parameters
    |
    ▼
stories render:
<ThemeProvider>
  <Story />
</ThemeProvider>
```

Hands-On Exercise

Objective: Configure and run Storybook, then add your first component story.

1. **Initialize Storybook:**
   - Run `npx sb init` and verify `.storybook` folder created.
2. **Configure `main.js`:**
   - Update `stories` globs, `addons`, and `webpackFinal` with your aliases.
3. **Configure `preview.js`:**
   - Import your global CSS (`index.css`) and wrap stories in `<ThemeProvider>`.
4. **Create a Story:**
   - In `src/components/atoms/Button/Button.stories.tsx`, write a basic story:
   - `import React from 'react';`

- `import { Button } from './Button';`
-
- `export default { title: 'Atoms/Button', component: Button };`
-
- `export const Primary = { args: { children: 'Click Me', variant: 'primary' } };`
- `export const Secondary = { args: { children: 'Cancel', variant: 'secondary' } };`

5. **Run and Verify:**
   - `npm run storybook`, navigate to `http://localhost:6006`, and confirm your Button stories render with correct styling and controls.

Key Takeaways

- Storybook CLI (`npx sb init`) bootstraps a working config.
- `main.js` defines story locations, addons, and build aliases.
- `preview.js` applies global decorators and parameters—wrapping stories in your design-system context and styles.

Next Steps
Proceed to **Section 5.2**, where we'll author rich MDX documentation and utilize the **Controls** addon to let readers interactively explore your component props.

5.2 Writing Stories: Args, Controls, and Docs-Page

Goal Statement
In this section you'll learn how to write component stories using Storybook's **args** and **controls** APIs and author rich documentation via the **Docs-Page** addon—making your components interactive, discoverable, and self-documenting.

Key Terms

- **Args**

- **Controls**
- **CSF (Component Story Format)**
- **Docs-Page**
- **MDX**

Practical Outcome
By the end, you'll create stories that define reusable default props (args), expose live controls for adjusting those props in the UI, and build a custom Docs-Page in MDX that combines examples, props tables, and usage guidelines.

Research & Gather Notes

- **Official Docs & Blogs**
  - Storybook "Args" and "Controls" documentation.
  - Storybook "Docs-Page" MDX guide.
- **Community Examples**
  - GitHub: Chakra UI's stories showcase controls and Docs-Page customization.
  - GitHub: Carbon Design System's MDX stories with code snippets and live playgrounds.
- **Your Own Experience**
  - Discovered that centralizing default args in `export default` simplifies component variants.
  - Learned that customizing Docs-Page via `parameters.docs.page` lets you mix Markdown and story functions seamlessly.

Storybook's **args** mechanism lets you define a component's props once and then reuse them across multiple stories, while **controls** automatically generate UI inputs—sliders, color pickers, selects—that let users tweak those props live. This interactivity transforms static examples into playgrounds, accelerating understanding and experimentation. Further, the **Docs-Page** addon uses the same args metadata to auto-generate prop tables and embed stories directly within Markdown or MDX, providing a comprehensive reference for each component.

We'll first author a Button story in **Component Story Format (CSF)**, defining default args and linking controls. Then we'll customize the Docs-Page to include an introductory description, the live component canvas, and a props table. Finally, we'll demonstrate how to embed additional MDX content—such as usage guidelines and code snippets—alongside the auto-generated documentation.

Concept Breakdown

1. **Args**
   - Reusable default prop values declared in `export default` under `args`.
   - Shared between stories and Docs-Page.
2. **Controls**
   - UI widgets in the "Controls" panel for live editing of args.
   - Auto-inferred from prop types or manually configured under `argTypes`.
3. **CSF (Component Story Format)**
   - Standard JS/TS format for writing stories: named exports correspond to stories.
4. **Docs-Page**
   - MDX-based documentation page that aggregates stories, descriptions, and prop tables.
   - Configured via `parameters.docs.page`.
5. **MDX**
   - Markdown for JSX: lets you mix Markdown and JSX to craft rich docs.

Code Walkthrough

```
// src/components/atoms/Button/Button.stories.tsx
import React from 'react';
import { Meta, Story } from '@storybook/react';
import { Button, ButtonProps } from './Button';

export default {
  title: 'Atoms/Button',
  component: Button,
  args: {
    children: 'Click Me',
    variant: 'primary',
    size: 'medium',
    disabled: false,
  },
  argTypes: {
    variant: {
      control: { type: 'radio' },
      options: ['primary', 'secondary'],
```

```
    },
    size: {
      control: { type: 'select' },
      options: ['small', 'medium', 'large'],
    },
    disabled: { control: 'boolean' },
  },
  parameters: {
    docs: {
      // use default DocsPage but add title & description
      page: () => (
        <>
          <h1>Button</h1>
          <p>A versatile button component supporting
variants, sizes, and disabled state.</p>
          <Story name="Primary" />
          <ArgsTable story="Primary" />
        </>
      ),
    },
  },
} as Meta<ButtonProps>;

const Template: Story<ButtonProps> = (args) => <Button
{...args} />;

export const Primary = Template.bind({});
export const Secondary = Template.bind({});
Secondary.args = { variant: 'secondary', children: 'Cancel'
};
export const Large = Template.bind({});
Large.args = { size: 'large', children: 'Large Button' };
```

- **What it does:**
  - Declares default args and control types in `export default`.
  - Creates a `Template` to bind multiple story variants.
  - Customizes the Docs-Page to include heading, description, and inline story with args table.
- **Why this approach:**
  - **DRY:** Args defined once propagate to stories and docs.
  - **Interactivity:** Controls panel reflects argTypes for live editing.
  - **Rich Docs:** MDX-style page blends narrative and live examples.

Common Pitfalls

1. **Missing ArgTypes**
   - Controls may show generic inputs if `argTypes` not defined.
   - **Fix:** Specify control types and options for enums or unions.
2. **Overly Complex Docs-Page**
   - Embedding too many manual elements duplicates autogenerated tables.
   - **Fix:** Leverage `<ArgsTable>` and `<Stories>` components for consistency.
3. **Inconsistent Default Args**
   - Default args may conflict with story-specific overrides.
   - **Fix:** Keep global defaults minimal; override per story only as needed.

```
Storybook Args & Controls Flow

export default {
  args: { variant: 'primary' },
  argTypes: { variant: { control: 'radio', options: [...] } }
}
         |
         ▼
<Story> – args ──▶ <Button variant="primary">
         |
         ▼
Controls Panel ←─ control changes ── update args ──▶ <Button
...>
```

Hands-On Exercise

Objective: Create interactive stories and a custom Docs-Page for your `<TextInput>` component.

1. **Define Args:**
   - In `TextInput.stories.tsx`, set default `label`, `value`, `placeholder`, and `error` under `args`.
2. **Configure Controls:**
   - Use `argTypes` to specify `error` as a boolean toggle and `placeholder` as a text control.
3. **Custom Docs-Page:**

    - Under `parameters.docs.page`, write an MDX function that introduces `TextInput`, shows the "Default" story, and renders `<ArgsTable>`.
4. **Verify:**
    - Run Storybook, open the TextInput Docs tab, confirm live controls and prop table.
5. **Deliverable:**
    - `TextInput.stories.tsx` with args, argTypes, and Docs-Page; screenshots of the Controls panel and Docs-Page layout.

Key Takeaways

- **Args** centralize default props; **Controls** generate live UI editors.
- **CSF** and **Template** patterns reduce boilerplate for multiple story variants.
- **Docs-Page** with MDX lets you combine narrative, live examples, and auto-generated prop tables.

Next Steps
Proceed to **Section 5.3**, where we'll add **automated visual regression testing** and integrate **Chromatic** to safeguard your design library against unintended style changes.

5.3 Automating Visual Regression Tests

Goal Statement
In this section you'll learn how to set up automated visual regression testing for your Storybook using tools like Chromatic or Percy—so that UI changes are caught early by comparing rendered component snapshots.

Key Terms

- **Visual Regression Testing**
- **Chromatic**
- **Snapshot Diff**
- **Baseline Build**
- **CI Integration**

Practical Outcome
By the end, you'll integrate a visual-testing service into your CI pipeline, publish your Storybook as a baseline "golden" UI reference, and enforce a check that flags any unintended UI changes on pull requests.

Research & Gather Notes

- **Official Docs & Blogs**
  - Chromatic: "Getting Started with Visual Testing."
  - Percy: "Visual Testing for Storybook" guide.
- **Community Examples**
  - GitHub: Storybook's Chromatic example repo.
  - GitHub Actions workflows that run `npx chromatic --project-token`.
- **Your Own Experience**
  - Found that integrating Chromatic uncovers layout shifts and CSS regressions that unit tests miss.
  - Learned to label review screenshots in PR comments for designer sign-off.

Manual UI review is tedious and error-prone. **Visual regression testing** tools capture images of each Storybook story in a baseline run, then compare future runs pixel-by-pixel, highlighting any differences. This approach ensures that style, spacing, typography, or structural changes don't slip through. We'll demonstrate Chromatic's free tier, which integrates seamlessly with Storybook and GitHub Actions, requiring only your project token and a CI step.

Once configured, each pull request triggers a Storybook build, uploads snapshots to Chromatic, and posts a report back to GitHub showing any regressions. Designers and developers can review diffs, approve intended changes, or reject regressions before merging—keeping your design system visually stable.

Concept Breakdown

1. **Visual Regression Testing**

    - Captures images of UI components and compares against a stored baseline.
2. **Baseline Build**
    - The initial upload of snapshots that establish the "correct" visual state.
3. **Snapshot Diff**
    - A pixel-level comparison highlighting new, removed, or changed pixels.
4. **CI Integration**
    - Automating the test run in GitHub Actions or other CI tools.
5. **Approval Workflow**
    - Team members review and accept or reject visual changes in the dashboard.

Code Walkthrough

```
# 1. Install the Chromatic CLI
npm install --save-dev chromatic

# 2. Add Chromatic script to package.json
"scripts": {
  "chromatic": "chromatic --project-token $CHROMATIC_TOKEN"
}
# .github/workflows/visual-regression.yml
name: Visual Regression

on: [pull_request]

jobs:
  test:
    runs-on: ubuntu-latest
    steps:
      - uses: actions/checkout@v3
      - name: Install dependencies
        run: npm ci
      - name: Build Storybook
        run: npm run build-storybook
      - name: Run Chromatic
        env:
          CHROMATIC_TOKEN: ${{ secrets.CHROMATIC_TOKEN }}
        run: npm run chromatic
```

- **What it does:**
    - Installs and runs Chromatic to capture Storybook snapshots.
    - Integrates with GitHub Actions to run on each PR.
- **Why this approach:**

    - **Catch UI Drift:** Automatically detect unintended changes.
    - **Collaborative Review:** Designers can approve visuals in Chromatic's UI.
    - **Peace of Mind:** Ensures your design system remains consistent over time.

Common Pitfalls

1. **Missing Token or Secrets**
    - Failing to set `CHROMATIC_TOKEN` in CI environment.
    - **Fix:** Store the token securely in your repository's secrets.
2. **Large Snapshot Count**
    - Very large component libraries can slow tests.
    - **Fix:** Group stories or exclude rarely-changed stories via flags.
3. **Flaky Stories**
    - Stories with non-deterministic content (timestamps, random data) cause false diffs.
    - **Fix:** Mock or stub dynamic data so snapshots are stable.

Chromatic CI Workflow

Pull Request →
Build Storybook
↓
Upload Snapshots
↓
Compare Baseline
↓
◄— Report Diffs —► Review & Approve

Hands-On Exercise

Objective: Integrate Chromatic into your design-system repo and run a visual test.

1. **Get Token:**
    - Sign up at chromatic.com, create a project, and copy the project token.
2. **Configure CI:**
    - Add `CHROMATIC_TOKEN` to your GitHub repo secrets.
    - Add the GitHub Actions workflow above.

3. **Run on PR:**
   - Open a PR with a story change (e.g., tweak Button padding).
   - Observe Chromatic's check status and view the diff report.
4. **Deliverable:**
   - A screenshot of the PR showing Chromatic workflow passing and diff report with highlighted changes.

Key Takeaways

- Visual regression testing captures UI snapshots and reports pixel-level changes.
- Chromatic integrates with Storybook and CI for automated checks on each pull request.
- Stable, deterministic stories and secure tokens are essential for reliable tests.

Next Steps
Proceed to **Section 5.4**, where we'll publish a live component catalog—deploying your Storybook to a public URL so stakeholders can browse and test your design system anywhere.

5.4 Publishing a Live Component Catalog

Goal Statement
In this section you'll learn how to deploy your Storybook as a publicly accessible component catalog—using services like GitHub Pages, Netlify, or Vercel—so stakeholders, designers, and developers can browse your design system anytime without installing anything locally.

Key Terms

- **Static Build**
- **Hosting Service**
- **Continuous Deployment (CD)**
- **Base Path**
- **Cache Invalidation**

Practical Outcome
By the end, you'll have an automated pipeline that builds your Storybook and publishes it to a live URL on every commit to your main branch—ensuring your component library is always up-to-date and shareable.

Research & Gather Notes

- **Official Docs & Blogs**
    - Storybook "Deploying to GitHub Pages" guide.
    - Netlify docs on "Continuous Deployment from Git."
    - Vercel docs on "Deploying Static Sites."
- **Community Examples**
    - GitHub: open-source projects with `.github/workflows/deploy-storybook.yml`.
    - GitHub: Netlify's `netlify.toml` for Storybook.
- **Your Own Experience**
    - Noted that setting the correct `--basePath` for Storybook avoids broken asset links.
    - Learned to configure cache headers on CD services to speed up repeated visits.

Publishing a live Storybook turns it into a living reference for your entire team—and even external stakeholders. You'll generate a static build of your Storybook (`npm run build-storybook`) and push it to a hosting service. With Continuous Deployment configured, every merge to your main branch triggers a fresh build and deploy, so your catalog always reflects the latest components, themes, and documentation.

We'll cover three common hosting options:

1. **GitHub Pages:** Free, integrates with GitHub Actions.
2. **Netlify:** Simple drag-and-drop or Git-connected deploys with painless redirects.
3. **Vercel:** Zero-config for most React apps, automatic previews and rollbacks.

Concept Breakdown

1. **Static Build**

   - `build-storybook` outputs an `storybook-static/` folder containing HTML, CSS, and JS.
2. **Hosting Service**
   - A CDN-backed platform that serves static assets under a public URL.
3. **Continuous Deployment (CD)**
   - Automated workflow: on push, build artifacts are redeployed without manual steps.
4. **Base Path**
   - If your site is served under a subpath (e.g. `yourdomain.com/design-system/`), Storybook needs `--basePath` or `--path` /design-system``.
5. **Cache Invalidation**
   - Ensuring browsers fetch the new build after changes—often managed by service defaults.

---

4. Code Walkthrough

A. GitHub Pages via Actions

```
# .github/workflows/deploy-storybook.yml
name: Deploy Storybook to GitHub Pages

on:
  push:
    branches: [ main ]

jobs:
  deploy:
    runs-on: ubuntu-latest
    steps:
      - uses: actions/checkout@v3
      - name: Install dependencies
        run: npm ci
      - name: Build Storybook
        run: npm run build-storybook -- --output-dir
storybook-static
      - name: Deploy to GitHub Pages
        uses: peaceiris/actions-gh-pages@v3
        with:
          github_token: ${{ secrets.GITHUB_TOKEN }}
          publish_dir: ./storybook-static
```

B. Netlify via `netlify.toml`

```
[build]
  command   = "npm run build-storybook"
  publish   = "storybook-static"
  base      = "/"

[[redirects]]
  from = "/*"
  to   = "/index.html"
  status = 200
```

C. Vercel via `vercel.json`

```
{
  "builds": [
    { "src": "package.json", "use": "@vercel/static-build",
"config": { "distDir": "storybook-static" } }
  ],
  "routes": [
    { "src": "/(.*)", "dest": "/index.html" }
  ]
}
```

- **What it does:**
  - Each snippet automates building and deploying your static Storybook to the chosen host.
- **Why this approach:**
  - **Reliability:** Every commit yields an updated live catalog.
  - **Accessibility:** Team members access components via a stable URL.
  - **Visibility:** Designers, QA, and stakeholders can review UI in isolation.

Hands-On Exercise

Objective: Deploy your Storybook to a live URL with CI.

1. **Choose Hosting:**
   - Pick GitHub Pages, Netlify, or Vercel for your project.
2. **Configure Build & Deploy:**
   - Add the appropriate config file (`deploy-storybook.yml`, `netlify.toml`, or `vercel.json`).

3. **Set Secrets & Settings:**
   - For GitHub Pages: ensure `gh-pages` branch protection and `GITHUB_TOKEN` are set.
   - For Netlify/Vercel: connect your Git repo and set build commands.
4. **Trigger Deployment:**
   - Push to `main`; monitor CI logs for build and deploy success.
5. **Deliverable:**
   - A live URL (e.g. `https://your-org.github.io/your-repo/`) showing your Storybook catalog.

Key Takeaways

- Use `npm run build-storybook` to generate the static catalog folder.
- Configure CI workflows or platform config files to deploy on every commit.
- Ensure correct base paths and redirects so Storybook assets resolve properly.

Next Steps
In **Chapter 6**, we'll shift focus to advanced patterns and architecture—exploring compound components, custom hooks, and performance optimizations to elevate your design system further.

Visual Aid: Storybook Configuration Table

Storybook Configuration Overview

File / Command	Purpose
npx sb init	Scaffold Storybook with webpack5 builder and essentials addon
.storybook/main.js	• stories: glob pattern for *.stories

	• addons: controls, docs, a11y, etc. • webpackFinal: set up import aliases
.storybook/preview.js	• decorators: wrap stories in <ThemeProvider> and global CSS • parameters: actions, controls, a11y
npm run storybook	Launch local Storybook at localhost:6006
npm run build-storybook	Generate static build in storybook-static
CI Workflow (GitHub) .github/workflows/...	• Checkout, npm ci, build-storybook • Deploy via Chromatic/Pages/Netlify

5.5 End-of-Chapter Summary & Key Takeaways

1. **Storybook Setup**
    - `npx sb init` bootstraps a Storybook environment.
    - Configure `.storybook/main.js` for your story globs, addons, and Webpack aliases.
    - Use `.storybook/preview.js` to import global CSS and wrap all stories in your `ThemeProvider`.
2. **Interactive Stories with Args & Controls**
    - Define reusable default props under `export default.args`.
    - Expose live controls via `argTypes` so users can tweak props in real time.
    - Craft rich MDX **Docs-Page** layouts combining narrative, live examples (`<Story>`), and prop tables (`<ArgsTable>`).
3. **Visual Regression Testing**
    - Integrate Chromatic (or Percy) to capture Storybook snapshots and detect unintended UI changes.
    - Automate via CI workflows (`npx chromatic --project-token`) to enforce visual consistency on every pull request.
4. **Publishing Your Catalog**

- Run `npm run build-storybook` to generate the static `storybook-static/` folder.
- Deploy automatically to GitHub Pages, Netlify, or Vercel with a simple CI/CD configuration.
- Ensure correct base paths and redirects so assets resolve properly in production.

— With Storybook configured, interactive, tested, and publicly hosted, your design system is now a living, shareable catalog. In Chapter 6, we'll explore **Advanced Patterns and Architecture**—diving into compound components, custom hooks, and performance optimizations to further mature your library.

5.6 Hands-On Exercises

Exercise 1: Create Stories for Core Components

- **Objective:** Write CSF stories with args and controls for three components.
- **Steps:**
  1. For `<Button>`, `<TextInput>`, and `<Checkbox>`, create `*.stories.tsx` files under their folders.
  2. In each default export, define `args` for the most common props (e.g., `variant`, `size`, `disabled`, `label`, `error`).
  3. Configure `argTypes` to expose appropriate controls (radio for enums, boolean for flags, text for strings).
  4. Use a `Template` and `.bind({})` pattern to create at least two variants per component.
- **Deliverable:** Story files showing interactive controls for each component in Storybook.

Exercise 2: Build a Custom Docs-Page for a Component

- **Objective:** Author a tailored documentation page in MDX for one of your molecules (e.g., `<Card>`).
- **Steps:**

1. Rename or add a `Card.stories.mdx` alongside `Card.stories.tsx`.
2. At the top, write a heading, a brief description of the component's purpose, and a list of usage guidelines.
3. Embed your CSF stories with <Story name="Default" /> and <Story name="With Actions" />.
4. Include <ArgsTable of={Meta} /> to auto-generate a props table.

- **Deliverable:** An MDX story page that combines narrative, live examples, and props documentation.

Exercise 3: Set Up and Validate Visual Regression

- **Objective:** Integrate Chromatic into your CI and validate a visual test run.
- **Steps:**
  1. Install `chromatic` and add a `chromatic` script in `package.json` with your project token.
  2. Create a GitHub Actions workflow (`.github/workflows/visual-regression.yml`) to run `npm run chromatic` on pull requests.
  3. Modify an existing story (e.g., change Button padding) and open a PR.
  4. Review the Chromatic report, confirm the diff is detected, and approve or reject the change.
- **Deliverable:** A PR showing the Chromatic workflow run and a screenshot of the diff report.

Exercise 4: Publish Storybook to a Live URL

- **Objective:** Automate deployment of your Storybook to a public host.
- **Steps:**
  1. Choose a hosting service (GitHub Pages, Netlify, or Vercel).
  2. Add the appropriate configuration (`deploy-storybook.yml`, `netlify.toml`, or `vercel.json`).
  3. Push to `main` and verify the build-and-deploy pipeline succeeds.

4. Share the live URL and navigate through your component catalog.

- **Deliverable:** A live link to your deployed Storybook and confirmation that new commits trigger automatic updates.

5.7 Next Steps: Integrating Chromatic

Goal Statement
In this section you'll learn how to wire up Chromatic's visual regression service to your existing Storybook setup—so that every pull request automatically captures snapshots, compares them to your baseline, and reports any unintended UI changes back to GitHub.

Key Terms

- **Chromatic Project Token**
- **Baseline Snapshot**
- **GitHub Actions**
- **Visual Diff Review**
- **Approval Workflow**

Practical Outcome
By the end, you'll have added a `chromatic` script, configured a GitHub Actions job, and verified that Chromatic runs on each pull request—flagging regressions and allowing your team to review and approve changes via Chromatic's dashboard.

Research & Gather Notes

- **Official Docs & Blogs**
    - Chromatic's "Getting Started" tutorial for Storybook.
    - Chromatic CLI reference on project tokens and flags.
- **Community Examples**
    - GitHub: Storybook's official Chromatic example repository.
    - GitHub Actions workflows demonstrating `npx chromatic --exit-zero-on-changes`.
- **Your Own Experience**

    - Found that setting `--exit-zero-on-changes` lets CI pass while still surfacing diffs.
    - Learned to annotate PRs with Chromatic's check run, linking directly to the visual diff.

Chromatic provides a seamless way to catch visual regressions by integrating directly with your Storybook. After installing the Chromatic CLI and adding your **project token**, you invoke `npx chromatic` during your CI build. Chromatic uploads your Storybook, captures "golden" baseline snapshots on the first run, and on subsequent runs compares new snapshots pixel-by-pixel. Any visual diffs appear in the Chromatic dashboard and as a status check on your pull request—letting designers and developers review and approve intended changes before merge.

To integrate Chromatic with GitHub Actions, you add a workflow step that runs your `chromatic` script and sets the `CHROMATIC_TOKEN` secret. You can pass flags—such as `--exit-zero-on-changes` to avoid blocking merges on diffs, or `--auto-accept-changes` if you prefer automatic baselines—to tailor the workflow to your team's process.

```
Chromatic Integration Flow

Pull Request ──▸ GitHub Actions ──▸ npx chromatic ──▸ Upload Storybook
                                          │
                                          ▼
                                  Chromatic Dashboard
                                          │
                  ┌──────── Approve ──────┴────── Reject ─────┐
                  ▼                                           ▼
          Merge (no regressions)                       Fix UI & update
```

Hands-On Exercise

Objective: Configure and validate Chromatic in your repo.

1. **Install and Script:**
    - `npm install --save-dev chromatic`
    - Add to `package.json`:

```
"scripts": {
  "chromatic": "chromatic --project-token $CHROMATIC_TOKEN --
exit-zero-on-changes"
}
```

2. **Set Secret:**

    - In GitHub repository settings, add `CHROMATIC_TOKEN` with your project token.
3. **Configure Workflow:**
    - Create `.github/workflows/visual-regression.yml`:

```
on: [pull_request]
jobs:
  chromatic:
    runs-on: ubuntu-latest
    steps:
      - uses: actions/checkout@v3
      - run: npm ci
      - run: npm run build-storybook
      - env:
          CHROMATIC_TOKEN: ${{ secrets.CHROMATIC_TOKEN }}
        run: npm run chromatic
```

4. **Validate:**
    - Open a PR that tweaks a component's style.
    - Observe the Chromatic check running and view the diff in the Chromatic dashboard.
    - Approve or reject the change to complete the check.

Key Takeaways

- Chromatic automates visual regression by uploading Storybook snapshots and reporting diffs.
- A simple `chromatic` script plus a GitHub Actions job enables CI-driven checks on every PR.
- Flags like `--exit-zero-on-changes` and `--auto-accept-changes` let you balance strictness and flexibility.

Next Steps
Proceed to **Chapter 6**, where we'll delve into **Advanced Patterns and Architecture**—exploring compound components, custom hooks, performance optimizations, and versioning strategies to further solidify and scale your React design system.

Chapter 6: Advanced Patterns and Architecture

6.1 Compound Components and Render Props

Goal Statement
In this section you'll learn how to build **compound components**—a pattern where a parent component manages state and multiple interchangeable child components consume that state—and how to expose that state via **render props**, enabling flexible, declarative APIs.

Key Terms

- **Compound Components**
- **Render Props**
- **Context API**
- **State Colocation**
- **Declarative Composition**

Practical Outcome
By the end, you'll implement a `<Tabs>` component with `<TabList>`, `<Tab>`, and `<TabPanels>` children that share selection state. You'll also build a `<Modal>` using a render-props `<ModalController>` to expose `open`/`close` methods and current `isOpen` flag to its children.

Research & Gather Notes

- **Official Docs & Blogs**
  - React docs: "Context" for sharing state across component trees.
  - Kent C. Dodds blog: "Compound Component Pattern in React."
- **Community Examples**
  - Reach UI's `Tabs` implementation using context.
  - Headless UI's `Tab.Group` compound API.
- **Your Own Experience**

- Found that combining compound components with render props yields maximum flexibility without prop drilling.
- Learned to document the API carefully so consumers know which child components to include under the parent.

Imagine a Tabs UI: you need to coordinate which tab is active, render the list of tab labels, and show the corresponding panel content. A **compound component** pattern lets you expose a single `<Tabs>` parent that internally manages selected index, while its children—`<TabList>`, `<Tab>`, `<TabPanels>`, `<TabPanel>`—automatically share that selection state. Consumer code reads as:

```
<Tabs defaultIndex={0}>
  <TabList>
    <Tab>Home</Tab>
    <Tab>Profile</Tab>
    <Tab>Settings</Tab>
  </TabList>
  <TabPanels>
    <TabPanel>Home content…</TabPanel>
    <TabPanel>Profile content…</TabPanel>
    <TabPanel>Settings content…</TabPanel>
  </TabPanels>
</Tabs>
```

Under the hood, `<Tabs>` uses React Context to provide `selectedIndex` and a `setSelectedIndex` callback. Each `<Tab>` subscribes via `useContext` and renders itself as active or not, invoking `setSelectedIndex` on click. This approach keeps state colocated, avoids prop drilling, and yields a clean, declarative API.

A similar pattern uses **render props**: instead of fixed child components, you pass a function as a child that receives controller props. For a Modal, you could write:

```
<ModalController>
  {({ isOpen, open, close }) => (
    <>
      <Button onClick={open}>Show modal</Button>
      {isOpen && (
        <Modal onClose={close}>
          {/* modal content */}
        </Modal>
      )}
    </>
  )}
</ModalController>
```

This pattern gives ultimate flexibility: consumers can decide exactly how and where to render UI, while the controller manages open/close state.

Concept Breakdown

1. **Compound Components**
   - Parent wraps children, provides shared state via Context.
   - Children read/write that context, requiring minimal props.
2. **Render Props**
   - Parent takes a function child, calls it with its internal state and actions.
   - Consumers render whatever they like based on provided API.
3. **State Colocation**
   - State lives in one place (the parent), preventing duplication and drift.
4. **Declarative Composition**
   - Consumers describe UI structure; library wires behavior under the hood.
5. **Context API**
   - Provides a lightweight mechanism for sharing state/actions across nested components.

Code Walkthrough

```
// Tabs.tsx
import React, { createContext, useContext, useState } from
'react';

interface TabsContext {
  selectedIndex: number;
  selectIndex: (i: number) => void;
}
const TabsContext = createContext<TabsContext | null>(null);

export function Tabs({ defaultIndex = 0, children }) {
  const [selectedIndex, selectIndex] =
useState(defaultIndex);
  return (
    <TabsContext.Provider value={{ selectedIndex, selectIndex
}}>
      {children}
    </TabsContext.Provider>
  );
}

export function TabList({ children }) {
```

```
  return <div role="tablist">{children}</div>;
}

export function Tab({ index, children }) {
  const ctx = useContext(TabsContext)!;
  const isSelected = ctx.selectedIndex === index;
  return (
    <button
      role="tab"
      aria-selected={isSelected}
      onClick={() => ctx.selectIndex(index)}
      style={{ fontWeight: isSelected ? 'bold' : 'normal' }}
    >
      {children}
    </button>
  );
}

export function TabPanels({ children }) {
  return <div>{children}</div>;
}

export function TabPanel({ index, children }) {
  const ctx = useContext(TabsContext)!;
  return ctx.selectedIndex === index ? (
    <div role="tabpanel">{children}</div>
  ) : null;
}
// ModalController.tsx
import React, { useState } from 'react';

export function ModalController({ children }) {
  const [isOpen, setOpen] = useState(false);
  const open = () => setOpen(true);
  const close = () => setOpen(false);
  return <>{children({ isOpen, open, close })}</>;
}
```

- **What it does:**
  - `<Tabs>` and related exports form a compound API using Context.
  - `<ModalController>` uses render props to expose its state/actions.
- **Why this approach:**
  - **Flexibility:** Consumers use provided child components (Tabs) or custom markup (Modal).
  - **Clarity:** Parent API surface is minimal; children handle UI specifics.

Common Pitfalls

1. **Missing Context Provider**
   - Forgetting to wrap children in `<Tabs>` causes `useContext` to return null.
   - **Fix:** Add runtime guard or throw a clear error if context is missing.
2. **Tight Coupling of Children Order**
   - Assuming children appear in a fixed order or count (e.g., Tab indices).
   - **Fix:** Derive `index` via `React.Children.map` so explicit `index` prop isn't required.
3. **Excessive Re-Renders**
   - Frequent context updates can re-render all descendants.
   - **Fix:** Memoize context value or split context for state vs. actions.

```
Tabs Compound Pattern

<Tabs>                                Context
  ├─ <TabList>                        ┌──────────────────────────────┐
  │     ├─ <Tab index=0> ◄────────────│ selectedIndex: 0             │
  │     └─ <Tab index=1>              │ selectIndex: fn              │
  └─ <TabPanels>                      └──────────────────────────────┘
        ├─ <TabPanel index=0> ▶ renders because
selectedIndex===0
        └─ <TabPanel index=1> ▶ hidden
```

Hands-On Exercise

Objective: Build a compound `<Accordion>` and a render-props `<ToggleController>`.

1. **Accordion:**
   - Create `Accordion`, `AccordionItem`, `AccordionHeader`, and `AccordionPanel` components.
   - Parent `<Accordion>` manages an `openIndex` state; each `<AccordionHeader>` toggles its panel via context.
2. **ToggleController:**
   - Implement `<ToggleController>` similar to `<ModalController>`, exposing `[isToggled, toggle]` to its function child.

    - Use it to build a "Read More" section that expands/collapses.
3. **Deliverable:**
    - Source files for both patterns and a small demo page rendering the Accordion and "Read More" section.

Key Takeaways

- **Compound components** colocate state in a parent and share it with named children via Context.
- **Render props** expose state and actions to function children, enabling custom UI.
- Both patterns provide highly flexible, declarative APIs without prop drilling.

Next Steps
Proceed to **Section 6.2**, where we'll explore **High-Order Components vs. Custom Hooks**—comparing patterns for code reuse and cross-cutting concerns in your design system.

6.2 High-Order Components vs. Custom Hooks

Goal Statement
In this section you'll learn when to use **High-Order Components (HOCs)** to wrap and enhance existing components versus **Custom Hooks** to encapsulate reusable logic—selecting the pattern that best fits your design-system needs for code reuse and separation of concerns.

Key Terms

- **High-Order Component (HOC)**
- **Custom Hook**
- **Cross-Cutting Concern**
- **Render Wrapping**
- **Logic Reuse**

Practical Outcome
By the end, you'll implement both an HOC (`withLoadingIndicator`) and a custom hook (`useLoading`) to share "loading" behavior across components, weigh trade-offs, and choose the right pattern for new cross-cutting concerns.

Research & Gather Notes

- **Official Docs & Blogs**
  - React docs: "Hooks at a Glance" and HOC patterns overview.
  - Kent C. Dodds: "When to use hooks vs. HOCs" blog post.
- **Community Examples**
  - GitHub: `react-redux`'s `connect` HOC vs. `useSelector` hook.
  - GitHub: `@reach/router` HOCs for route props vs. `useLocation` hook.
- **Your Own Experience**
  - Noted that HOCs can obscure component trees in DevTools, whereas hooks keep the component identity clear.
  - Learned that custom hooks cannot modify JSX behavior—they only return data and callbacks, whereas HOCs can inject render logic.

When you need to apply the same behavior—such as data fetching, theming, or analytics—to multiple components, you can either wrap them in a **High-Order Component (HOC)** that injects props and render logic, or extract the logic into a **Custom Hook** that each component calls. HOCs take a component as input and return an enhanced component, whereas hooks return values and functions for use inside your component's body.

Use HOCs when you need to modify rendering—e.g., display a loading spinner in place of the wrapped component. Use custom hooks when you only need shared data, state, or side-effect logic, leaving the component's JSX unaffected. Choosing the right pattern keeps your component API predictable and your codebase maintainable.

Concept Breakdown

1. **High-Order Component (HOC)**
   - A function `withX(Component)` that returns a new component wrapping `Component`, often injecting additional props or rendering behavior.
2. **Custom Hook**

    - A function `useX()` that encapsulates stateful logic using React's built-in hooks, returning values and callbacks for the calling component.
3. **Cross-Cutting Concern**
    - Behavior needed by many components (e.g., loading states, error handling, feature flags).
4. **Render Wrapping**
    - HOCs can wrap and replace entire JSX trees (e.g., show a spinner), while hooks cannot alter JSX structure directly.
5. **Logic Reuse**
    - Hooks excel at reusing stateful logic; HOCs excel at reusing render patterns.

---

4. Code Walkthrough

```
// withLoadingIndicator.tsx (HOC)
import React from 'react';
import { useLoading } from '../hooks/useLoading';

export function withLoadingIndicator<P>(
  WrappedComponent: React.ComponentType<P>
) {
  return function WithLoading(props: P) {
    const { isLoading } = useLoading();
    if (isLoading) {
      return <div className="spinner">Loading...</div>;
    }
    return <WrappedComponent {...props} />;
  };
}
// useLoading.ts (Custom Hook)
import { useState, useEffect } from 'react';

export function useLoading() {
  const [isLoading, setLoading] = useState(true);
  useEffect(() => {
    const timer = setTimeout(() => setLoading(false), 1000);
    return () => clearTimeout(timer);
  }, []);
  return { isLoading };
}
```

- **What it does:**

- HOC: Wraps any component to show a spinner while `useLoading` indicates loading.
    - **Hook:** Manages a simple loading state and lifecycle without dictating rendering.
- **Why this approach:**
    - **HOC:** Ideal when you want to layer behavior that affects the component's JSX output uniformly.
    - **Hook:** Ideal for sharing stateful logic while leaving rendering decisions to each component.

Common Pitfalls

1. **Props Collision in HOCs**
    - HOCs may override or conflict with existing props on the wrapped component.
    - **Fix:** Pick unique prop names or use a prop namespace (`loadingState`).
2. **Component Wrapping Obscures DevTools**
    - Many nested HOCs make the component tree harder to read.
    - **Fix:** Use `displayName` on HOCs to clarify names (e.g., `WithLoading(MyComponent)`).
3. **Hooks Cannot Wrap Render Logic**
    - You can't return JSX from a hook—only data and callbacks.
    - **Fix:** Use HOCs or render-props for JSX-level concerns.

```
HOC vs. Hook Comparison

[withLoadingIndicator(MyComponent)]
  ├─ uses useLoading() internally
  └─ wraps JSX: shows spinner or renders MyComponent

MyComponent:
function MyComponent() {
  const { isLoading } = useLoading();
  return isLoading ? <Spinner /> : <Content />;
}
```

Hands-On Exercise

Objective: Share "error handling" behavior via both patterns.

1. **Build `useErrorHandler` Hook:**
   - Create a custom hook that calls a callback on error and tracks an `error` state.
2. **Build `withErrorBoundary` HOC:**
   - Create an HOC that wraps a component in a React error boundary, displaying a fallback UI on error.
3. **Compare Usage:**
   - Use `useErrorHandler` inside a component to catch errors in an effect.
   - Wrap another component with `withErrorBoundary` to catch render-time errors.
4. **Deliverable:**
   - Source for `useErrorHandler.ts` and `withErrorBoundary.tsx`, plus a demo showing both patterns in action.

Key Takeaways

- **HOCs** wrap and modify rendering, suitable for cross-cutting JSX concerns like spinners or error boundaries.
- **Custom Hooks** encapsulate reusable state and side-effect logic without dictating UI.
- Select the pattern that aligns with whether you need to alter rendering (HOC) or just share logic (hook).

Next Steps
Proceed to **Section 6.3**, where we'll explore **Performance Optimization: Memoization and Lazy Loading**, ensuring your design-system components stay performant as they grow.

6.3 Performance Optimization: Memoization and Lazy Loading

Goal Statement
In this section you'll learn how to boost your React design-system's performance by applying **memoization** (to avoid unnecessary renders) and **lazy loading** (to split code and defer loading until needed).

Key Terms

- **React.memo**
- **useMemo**
- **useCallback**
- **React.lazy**
- **Suspense**

Practical Outcome
By the end, you'll know how to wrap components with `React.memo`, cache expensive computations with `useMemo/useCallback`, and configure dynamic imports with `React.lazy` and `<Suspense>`—resulting in faster initial loads and fewer wasted renders.

Research & Gather Notes

- **Official Docs & Blogs**
  - React docs: "Optimizing Performance" chapter (memo, lazy, Suspense).
  - Dan Abramov blog on "useMemo and useCallback Gotchas."
- **Community Examples**
  - GitHub: Material-UI's lazy-loaded icons and memoized list items.
  - GitHub: `react-window` virtualization using memoized row renderers.
- **Your Own Experience**
  - Discovered that wrapping pure presentational components with `React.memo` cuts re-renders when their props don't change.
  - Learned that overusing `useMemo` can actually harm performance; it's best for expensive calculations.

As your component library grows, rendering complex lists or charts can become a performance bottleneck. **Memoization** tells React to skip re-rendering a component or recomputing a value when its inputs haven't changed. Meanwhile, **lazy loading** defers the download and execution of rarely used components—such as modals or icon sets—until they're actually rendered, shrinking your initial bundle.

We'll demonstrate `React.memo` for wrapping a pure `<Card>` so it only re-renders on prop changes, and show how `useMemo/useCallback` prevent child components from receiving new references unnecessarily. Then we'll refactor a heavy component—say an icon library—into a dynamic import via `React.lazy` and render it inside `<Suspense>`, complete with a fallback spinner.

Concept Breakdown

1. **React.memo**
   - Higher-order wrapper: `React.memo(Component)` will shallow-compare props and skip re-render if unchanged.
2. **useMemo**
   - Caches the result of an expensive function: `const value = useMemo(() => computeExpensive(a, b), [a, b]).`
3. **useCallback**
   - Caches a function reference: `const onClick = useCallback(() => doSomething(x), [x]).`
4. **React.lazy**
   - Allows dynamic import of components: `const LazyComponent = React.lazy(() => import('./Heavy')).`
5. **Suspense**
   - Boundary for lazy-loaded components: wraps with `<Suspense fallback={<Spinner/>}>.`

Code Walkthrough

```
// Memoizing a list item
import React from 'react';

interface CardProps { title: string; content: string; }
export const Card = React.memo<CardProps>(({ title, content
}) => {
  console.log('Rendering', title);
  return (
    <div className="card">
      <h3>{title}</h3>
      <p>{content}</p>
    </div>
```

```
  );
});
// Caching computation and callbacks
import React, { useMemo, useCallback } from 'react';

function List({ items }: { items: number[] }) {
  const sorted = useMemo(() => items.sort((a,b)=>a-b),
[items]);
  const handleClick = useCallback((item:number) => {
    console.log('Clicked', item);
  }, []);
  return (
    <ul>
      {sorted.map(i => (
        <li key={i}>
          <button onClick={() => handleClick(i)}>{i}</button>
        </li>
      ))}
    </ul>
  );
}
// Lazy-loading a heavy icon set
import React, { Suspense } from 'react';
const IconSet = React.lazy(() => import('./IconSet'));

export function IconGallery() {
  return (
    <Suspense fallback={<div>Loading icons…</div>}>
      <IconSet />
    </Suspense>
  );
}
```

- **What it does:**
  - `React.memo` skips re-render when props are the same.
  - `useMemo`/`useCallback` preserve references between renders.
  - `React.lazy` defers loading until first render; `Suspense` shows a fallback.
- **Why this approach:**
  - **Performance:** Reduces CPU work and bundle size.
  - **Responsiveness:** Faster initial page load, fewer wasted updates.

Common Pitfalls

1. **Over-Memoization**
   - Wrapping every component adds comparison overhead.
   - **Fix:** Only memoize pure, frequently re-rendered components.
2. **Incorrect Dependencies**
   - Omitting dependencies in `useMemo/useCallback` leads to stale values.
   - **Fix:** Always list all external values used inside the hook.
3. **Suspense Boundaries Too Far Down**
   - Placing `<Suspense>` inside deep trees causes multiple fallsbacks.
   - **Fix:** Wrap at a higher level to group lazy imports under one fallback.

```
Render Flow with Memo & Lazy

Initial Render:
[App]
 ├─ <Card title="A"/> (renders)
 ├─ <IconGallery>
 │     Suspense -> fallback
 └─ <OtherComponents>

Update (props unchanged):
[App]
 ├─ <Card title="A"/> (skipped by React.memo)
 ├─ <IconGallery> (IconSet already loaded)
```

Hands-On Exercise

Objective: Optimize a component-heavy page with memoization and lazy loading.

1. **Identify Candidate:**
   - Pick a component (e.g., `<Card>` list or icon library) that re-renders or is large.
2. **Apply Memoization:**
   - Wrap the pure component with `React.memo`.
   - Use `useMemo/useCallback` in its parent to stabilize props/callbacks.
3. **Implement Lazy Loading:**
   - Refactor the heavy component into a dynamic import via `React.lazy`.
   - Add a `<Suspense>` boundary in the parent with a fallback.

4. **Measure Impact:**
    - Use React DevTools Profiler to compare render counts before and after.
    - Note initial bundle size with and without lazy loading (`source-map-explorer`).
5. **Deliverable:**
    - Updated source files, Profiler screenshots showing reduced renders, and bundle size report.

Key Takeaways

- **React.memo** and **useMemo/useCallback** prevent unnecessary renders and recomputations.
- **React.lazy** and **Suspense** split code and defer loading of heavy components.
- Measure actual performance impact with DevTools and bundle analyzers.

Next Steps
Proceed to **Section 6.4**, where we'll cover **Versioning and Changelog Best Practices**—ensuring your design system evolves predictably and communicates changes clearly to consumers.

6.4 Versioning and Changelog Best Practices

Goal Statement
In this section you'll learn how to apply **semantic versioning** to your design-system releases, maintain a clear **changelog**, and automate release workflows—so that consumers can upgrade safely and understand what's changed in each version.

Key Terms

- **Semantic Versioning (SemVer)**
- **Changelog**
- **Breaking Change**
- **Patch, Minor, Major**
- **Automated Releases**

Practical Outcome
By the end, you'll be able to assign correct SemVer versions (e.g. `1.4.0` → minor, `2.0.0` → major), write clear changelog entries following Keep a Changelog conventions, and set up an automated GitHub Actions workflow to generate release notes and publish packages.

Research & Gather Notes

- **Official Docs & Blogs**
  - semver.org specification.
  - "Keep a Changelog" guidelines at keepachangelog.com.
- **Community Examples**
  - GitHub: `lerna` and `changesets` workflows for monorepos.
  - GitHub: `semantic-release` automated-release pipelines.
- **Your Own Experience**
  - Found that neglecting to bump the minor version for new features leads to consumer confusion.
  - Learned that generating changelogs via conventional commits saves time and ensures consistency.

As your design system grows and teams rely on it, managing releases systematically becomes critical. **Semantic Versioning (SemVer)** uses a three-part number—`MAJOR.MINOR.PATCH`—to communicate the nature of changes: patches for bug fixes, minors for new backward-compatible features, and majors for breaking API changes. A well-maintained **changelog** documents each release, giving consumers the context to decide when and how to upgrade.

Manually updating versions and writing release notes is error-prone. Tools like **semantic-release** or **changesets** automate version bumps, changelog generation, and package publishing based on commit messages. By adopting **Conventional Commits** (e.g. `feat: add new Button variant`, `fix: correct token mapping`, `BREAKING CHANGE: rename spacing keys`), you can automate the entire release workflow, ensuring every merge to `main` results in a correctly versioned release with generated release notes.

Concept Breakdown

1. **Semantic Versioning**

    - `PATCH`: backward-compatible bug fixes.
    - `MINOR`: backward-compatible features and improvements.
    - `MAJOR`: breaking API changes requiring consumer adjustments.
2. **Changelog**
    - A human-readable log with sections for each version (`## [1.2.0] - 2025-07-02`).
    - Follows "Keep a Changelog" format: Added, Changed, Deprecated, Removed, Fixed, Security.
3. **Conventional Commits**
    - Structured commit messages (`type(scope): description`).
    - Types: `feat`, `fix`, `docs`, `chore`, `refactor`, with optional `!` for breaking.
4. **Automated Releases**
    - Tools parse commit history, determine next version, update `package.json`, and publish.
5. **Release Workflow**
    - Merge → CI builds → release tool runs → version bump + changelog + publish.

---

4. Code Walkthrough

```
# Example GitHub Action: .github/workflows/release.yml
name: Release

on:
  push:
    branches: [ main ]

jobs:
  semantic-release:
    runs-on: ubuntu-latest
    steps:
      - uses: actions/checkout@v3
      - name: Install
        run: npm ci
      - name: Release
        env:
          GITHUB_TOKEN: ${{ secrets.GITHUB_TOKEN }}
          NPM_TOKEN: ${{ secrets.NPM_TOKEN }}
        run: npx semantic-release
// package.json (snippet)
{
```

```
  "release": {
    "branches": ["main"],
    "plugins": [
      "@semantic-release/commit-analyzer",
      "@semantic-release/release-notes-generator",
      ["@semantic-release/changelog", {
        "changelogFile": "CHANGELOG.md"
      }],
      "@semantic-release/npm",
      "@semantic-release/github"
    ]
  }
}
```

- **What it does:**
  - On every push to `main`, `semantic-release` reads commits, calculates the next SemVer, updates `CHANGELOG.md`, bumps `package.json`, and publishes to npm and GitHub Releases.
- **Why this approach:**
  - **Reliability:** Eliminates human error in versioning.
  - **Transparency:** Teams see precise, consistent changelogs.
  - **Efficiency:** Speeds up release process and enforces conventions.

Common Pitfalls

1. **Inconsistent Commit Messages**
   - Non-conventional commits break automation.
   - **Fix:** Enforce via a commit-lint hook (e.g. `@commitlint/cli`).
2. **Publishing Sensitive Files**
   - Accidentally including `.env` or test artifacts.
   - **Fix:** Use a curated `files` field in `package.json` or `.npmignore`.
3. **Not Handling Breaking Changes Properly**
   - Failing to signal breaking changes prevents a major bump.
   - **Fix:** Add `!` after type (`feat!:`) or include "BREAKING CHANGE:" in the commit body.

```
Release Pipeline Flow

Merge to main
     |
     ▼
```

```
CI: npm ci
      │
      ▼
CI: semantic-release
      │
      ▼
Determine next version
      │
      ▼
Update package.json & CHANGELOG.md
      │
      ▼
Publish to npm & GitHub Releases
```

Hands-On Exercise

Objective: Automate your design-system releases.

1. **Set Up Conventional Commits:**
   - Install `commitlint` and add a commit-lint Git hook enforcing `@commitlint/config-conventional`.
2. **Install Semantic-Release:**
   - **`npm install --save-dev semantic-release @semantic-release/npm @semantic-release/github @semantic-release/changelog @semantic-release/commit-analyzer @semantic-release/release-notes-generator.`**
3. **Configure `package.json`:**
   - Add `release` section with plugins (as above).
4. **Create GitHub Action:**
   - Add `.github/workflows/release.yml` to run `npx semantic-release` on pushes to `main`.
5. **Verify:**
   - Merge a `feat:` commit → observe CI bump minor version and update `CHANGELOG.md`.
   - Merge a `fix:` commit → patch bump.
   - Merge a `feat!:` or commit with `BREAKING CHANGE:` → major bump.

Key Takeaways

- **SemVer** communicates change impact via MAJOR.MINOR.PATCH.
- **Changelogs** following "Keep a Changelog" give clear release notes.
- **Automation** via `semantic-release` and commit conventions removes manual errors and speeds up your workflow.

Next Steps
Proceed to **Chapter 7**, where we'll cover **Integrating into Real Projects**—demonstrating how to consume your published design-system package, migrate existing codebases, and manage monorepos for large-scale adoption.

Visual Aid: Performance Optimization Checklist

```
Performance Optimization Checklist

┌─────────────────────────────────────────────────┐
│ [ ] Identify Pure Components                    │
│     • Wrap with React.memo                      │
│                                                 │
│ [ ] Cache Expensive Computations                │
│     • useMemo for derived values                │
│     • useCallback for event handlers            │
│                                                 │
│ [ ] Implement Code Splitting                    │
│     • React.lazy for heavy components           │
│     • Group related imports in dynamic chunks   │
│                                                 │
│ [ ] Add Suspense Boundaries                     │
│     • Wrap lazy-loaded components in Suspense   │
│     • Provide meaningful fallback UI            │
│                                                 │
│ [ ] Measure & Validate                          │
│     • Use React DevTools Profiler               │
│     • Analyze bundle with source-map-explorer   │
└─────────────────────────────────────────────────┘
```

6.5 End-of-Chapter Summary & Key Takeaways

1. **Compound Components & Render Props**
   - Colocate shared state in a parent and expose it via Context to named child components (`<Tabs>` family) or via render-prop controllers (`<ModalController>`).
   - Enables declarative, flexible APIs without prop drilling.
2. **High-Order Components vs. Custom Hooks**

   - **HOCs** wrap and enhance a component's rendering (e.g., `withLoadingIndicator`), ideal for injecting UI patterns.
   - **Custom Hooks** encapsulate reusable stateful logic (e.g., `useLoading`), ideal for sharing data and side effects without altering JSX.
3. **Performance Optimization**
   - **Memoization:** Use `React.memo`, `useMemo`, and `useCallback` judiciously to prevent unnecessary renders and expensive recomputations.
   - **Lazy Loading:** Leverage `React.lazy` and `<Suspense>` to defer loading of heavy or seldom-used components, shrinking initial bundle size.
4. **Versioning & Changelog Best Practices**
   - Adopt **Semantic Versioning (SemVer)**—PATCH for fixes, MINOR for backward-compatible features, MAJOR for breaking changes.
   - Maintain a clear **CHANGELOG.md** following "Keep a Changelog" conventions.
   - Automate releases with tools like **semantic-release** driven by Conventional Commits to ensure accurate version bumps and release notes.

With these advanced patterns and infrastructure in place, your design system is robust, maintainable, and performant—ready to scale across multiple projects and teams. Next, we'll put it all into practice by integrating the system into real applications in Chapter 7.

6.6 Hands-On Exercises

Exercise 1: Build a Compound Accordion

- **Objective:** Practice the compound component pattern by creating an accessible `<Accordion>` with shared state.
- **Steps:**
  1. Create `Accordion.tsx`, `AccordionItem.tsx`, `AccordionHeader.tsx`, and `AccordionPanel.tsx`.
  2. In `<Accordion>`, use `useState` to track `openIndex` and provide `{ openIndex, setOpenIndex }` via React Context.

3. In `<AccordionHeader>`, consume the context and toggle its panel on click.
4. In `<AccordionPanel>`, render its children only when its `index` matches `openIndex`.

- **Deliverable:** A demo page showing three accordion items, each opening and closing independently, with proper ARIA roles (`button`, `region`).

Exercise 2: Share "Error State" via HOC and Hook

- **Objective:** Compare HOC vs. custom hook approaches by adding error-handling behavior to two different components.
- **Steps:**
  1. Implement `useErrorState` hook that manages an `errorMessage` state and exposes a `setError` callback.
  2. Create `withErrorBoundary` HOC that wraps any component in an error boundary class, rendering a fallback UI if an error is thrown.
  3. Apply `useErrorState` inside a form component to capture validation errors and display them below inputs.
  4. Wrap a different component (e.g. a data-fetching widget) with `withErrorBoundary` so any render-time error shows a "Something went wrong" UI.
- **Deliverable:** Two components—one using the hook, one using the HOC—with screenshots demonstrating each error-handling pattern.

Exercise 3: Optimize and Lazy-Load a Heavy Component

- **Objective:** Improve performance by memoizing a list and lazy-loading an icon gallery.
- **Steps:**
  1. Identify a pure list component (e.g. `<CardList>` rendering dozens of cards) and wrap it with `React.memo`. Measure re-render counts with React DevTools Profiler.
  2. Refactor any expensive calculation inside it to use `useMemo`.

3. Move a heavy component (e.g. an icon set or chart) into a separate file and import it via `React.lazy`, wrapping it in `<Suspense>` with a spinner fallback.
4. Re-run the Profiler and note reduced initial bundle size and fewer wasted renders.

- **Deliverable:** Updated code, Profiler screenshots showing before/after render metrics, and bundle analysis report showing code-splitting effect.

Exercise 4: Automate a Patch Release with Conventional Commits

- **Objective:** Set up an automated release for a bug fix using conventional commits and semantic-release.
- **Steps:**
  1. Install and configure `commitlint` with `@commitlint/config-conventional` and Husky pre-commit hook.
  2. Make a small fix in a component, commit with a message like `fix(button): correct disabled styling.`
  3. Merge to `main` and let your CI run `semantic-release`—verify that `package.json` version increments PATCH, `CHANGELOG.md` updates, and a GitHub Release is published.
- **Deliverable:** A link to the GitHub Release page showing the new patch version and changelog entry for the fix.

6.7 Next Steps: Benchmarking Your Library

Goal Statement
In this section you'll learn how to measure and monitor your design-system's performance—both at build time (bundle size) and at runtime (render costs)—so you can identify bottlenecks, track improvements, and ensure consistent user experience as your library evolves.

Key Terms

- **Bundle Analysis**
- **Runtime Profiling**
- **Lighthouse**
- **Performance Budget**

- **Regression Monitoring**

Practical Outcome
By the end, you'll be able to generate bundle-size reports, run runtime performance benchmarks via React Profiler and Lighthouse, set performance budgets, and integrate these checks into CI to catch regressions early.

Research & Gather Notes

- **Official Docs & Blogs**
  - Webpack Bundle Analyzer guide.
  - React DevTools Profiler documentation.
  - Google Lighthouse performance audit docs.
- **Community Examples**
  - GitHub: Next.js performance budgets in CI with `size-limit`.
  - Blog: "How we measure component library performance" from open-source UI frameworks.
- **Your Own Experience**
  - Found that adding a `performanceBudget` step to CI prevents uncontrolled growth.
  - Learned to script Lighthouse CLI runs and parse JSON reports for key metrics.

Benchmarking your library involves two dimensions:

1. **Build-Time Metrics**
   - **Bundle Analysis:** Tools like **webpack-bundle-analyzer** or **source-map-explorer** reveal which modules contribute most to your package size. Identifying large dependencies or duplicated code lets you refactor or lazy-load accordingly.
2. **Runtime Metrics**
   - **React Profiler:** Captures "commit" and "render" timings per component interaction, showing which components consume the most time.
   - **Lighthouse Audits:** Provides overall page/performance scores, including First Contentful Paint and Time to Interactive, giving an external gauge of user experience.

By combining these, you can set a **performance budget**—for example, "total bundle ≤ 200 KB minified" or "no component render exceeding 5 ms"—and enforce it via automated CI checks. Over time, these benchmarks help you spot regressions and quantify the impact of new features.

```
Benchmarking Workflow

[Build]
    │
    ├─ webpack-bundle-analyzer → Bundle Report
    │
[CI Check] ← size-limit (200 KB max)
    │
[Runtime]
    │
    ├─ React Profiler → Render Flamechart
    │
    └─ Lighthouse CLI → Performance Score
```

Hands-On Exercise

Objective: Establish benchmarking for your design system.

1. **Bundle Analysis:**
   - Install `source-map-explorer` (`npm install --save-dev source-map-explorer`).
   - Add `"analyze": "source-map-explorer dist/index.js"` to `package.json`.
   - Build your library and run `npm run analyze`; inspect the file-size breakdown.
2. **Size Budget:**
   - Install `size-limit` and `@size-limit/preset-small-lib`.
   - Configure `.size-limit.js` with your bundle entry and budget (e.g., 200 KB).
   - Add `npm run size` script and verify it passes locally.
3. **Runtime Profiling:**
   - Wrap a demo page in React Profiler (`<Profiler>`) and interact with your components.
   - Record the slowest commits and identify hotspots.
4. **Lighthouse Audit:**
   - Install `lighthouse` CLI globally.

   - Run `lighthouse http://localhost:3000 --quiet --chrome-flags="--headless" --output=json --output-path=lh-report.json`.
   - Review metrics like FCP and TTI.
5. **CI Integration:**
   - Add a GitHub Action step to run `npm run size` and fail on budget breach.
   - Optionally, run Lighthouse in CI and upload the report as an artifact.

Deliverable:

- Bundle report screenshot.
- `size-limit` config and a passing CI check.
- Profiler flamechart snippet highlighting the top render cost.
- Lighthouse summary JSON or HTML report.

Key Takeaways

- **Build-Time:** Use bundle analyzers and size budgets to control package growth.
- **Runtime:** Leverage React Profiler and Lighthouse for in-depth performance insights.
- **Automation:** Integrate these benchmarks into CI to prevent regressions and maintain a high-quality design system.

Next Steps

Proceed to **Chapter 7**, where we'll demonstrate **Integrating into Real Projects**—showing how to consume your published library, migrate legacy code, and manage monorepos for large-scale adoption.

Chapter 7: Integrating into Real Projects

7.1 Consuming Your Library in a Create React App

Goal Statement
In this section you'll learn how to install, configure, and import your published design-system package into a new Create React App (CRA) project—verifying that your components, tokens, and Storybook decorators work seamlessly in a consumer application.

Key Terms

- **Create React App (CRA)**
- **npm / Yarn**
- **Peer Dependencies**
- **CSS Variable Imports**
- **Module Resolution**

Practical Outcome
By the end, you'll have a fresh CRA scaffold that consumes your `@your-org/design-system` package, applies global styles and theme provider, and renders a sample page using your components without additional hacks.

Research & Gather Notes

- **Official Docs & Blogs**
  - Create React App "Adding a Library" guide.
  - npm documentation on installing and managing peer dependencies.
- **Community Examples**
  - GitHub: consuming `@chakra-ui/react` in a CRA sandbox.
  - GitHub: Storybook decorators applied in consumer apps.
- **Your Own Experience**
  - Noted that forgetting to import CSS variables can result in unstyled components.
  - Learned to configure CRA's `jsconfig.json` for import path aliases matching your library.

Once you've published your design system to npm—or a private registry—teams should be able to consume it in any React project with minimal friction. A Create React App provides a common baseline: zero-config build, hot reload, and TypeScript support (if desired). We'll demonstrate installing your library, configuring global CSS imports, adding optional aliases, and rendering a sample component.

Concept Breakdown

1. **Installation**
   - Use `npm install @your-org/design-system` (and `npm install --save-dev` for any peerDeps like `styled-components`, if your library uses them).
2. **Peer Dependencies**
   - Ensure your CRA project has matching React, ReactDOM, and styling-library versions to avoid duplicate instances.
3. **Global CSS & Tokens**
   - Import your library's `styles/index.css` (or equivalent) in `src/index.js` before rendering the app so CSS variables and fonts are available.
4. **Importing Components**
   - Consume components via named imports:
   - `import { Button, TextInput, ThemeProvider } from '@your-org/design-system';`
5. **Aliases (Optional)**
   - Mirror your library's internal aliases in the consumer's `jsconfig.json` or `tsconfig.json` to support absolute imports.

Code Walkthrough

```
# 1. Scaffold a new CRA project
npx create-react-app consumer-app --template cra-template-pwa

cd consumer-app

# 2. Install your design-system package (and peer deps)
npm install @your-org/design-system styled-components

# 3. Verify peer dependencies
npm ls react react-dom styled-components
// src/index.js
import React from 'react';
import ReactDOM from 'react-dom';
```

```
import { ThemeProvider } from '@your-org/design-system';
import '@your-org/design-system/styles/index.css'; // CSS
variables & global styles
import App from './App';

ReactDOM.render(
  <ThemeProvider>
    <App />
  </ThemeProvider>,
  document.getElementById('root')
);
// src/App.js
import React from 'react';
import { Button, TextInput, Container } from '@your-
org/design-system';

function App() {
  return (
    <Container>
      <h1>Consumer App</h1>
      <TextInput label="Name" placeholder="Your name" />
      <Button variant="primary" onClick={() =>
alert('Hello!')}>
        Say Hello
      </Button>
    </Container>
  );
}

export default App;
```

- **What it does:**
    - Sets up CRA, installs your library and its peer dependencies.
    - Imports global CSS and wraps the app in `ThemeProvider`.
    - Renders core components to verify styles and functionality.
- **Why this approach:**
    - **Minimal friction:** Teams simply run `npm install` and import.
    - **Consistency:** Consumer apps automatically use your design-system tokens and themes.

Common Pitfalls

1. **Missing Global Styles**
    - Forgetting `styles/index.css` import leads to unstyled components.

- Fix: Always import your library's CSS entry in the root file before any component usage.

2. **Peer Dependency Mismatch**
   - Installing a different React version than your library causes duplicate contexts or hooks errors.
   - **Fix:** Align React, ReactDOM, and styling-library versions between projects.
3. **Path Aliases Not Resolved**
   - Absolute imports from your library (e.g. `styles/tokens`) fail.
   - **Fix:** Add matching `baseUrl` and `paths` in `jsconfig.json` or `tsconfig.json`.

```
Consumer App Initialization

npx create-react-app consumer-app
      |
npm install @your-org/design-system styled-components
      |
src/index.js ──▶
  import styles/index.css
  <ThemeProvider>
    <App />
  </ThemeProvider>
      |
src/App.js ──▶ uses <Button>, <TextInput>, <Container>
```

Hands-On Exercise

Objective: Integrate and verify your design system in a fresh CRA.

1. **Scaffold and Install:**
   - Run `npx create-react-app` and install `@your-org/design-system` plus any peer dependencies.
2. **Global Setup:**
   - In `src/index.js`, import your library's global CSS and wrap `<App>` with `<ThemeProvider>`.
3. **Render Sample Components:**
   - In `App.js`, import and render at least three components: one atom (`<Button>`), one molecule (`<TextInput>`), and one layout primitive (`<Container>`).

4. **Verify:**
    - Start the app (`npm start`) and ensure all components appear styled and interactive.
    - Check console warnings for missing peers or version mismatches.
5. **Deliverable:**
    - Screenshot of the running CRA with your components.
    - Console log confirming no peer-dependency errors.

Key Takeaways

- Installing your design system in CRA requires adding both your package and its peer dependencies.
- Import global CSS and wrap in `ThemeProvider` at the root to enable tokens and theming.
- Verify component rendering and watch for version mismatches or missing style imports.

Next Steps
Proceed to **Section 7.2**, where we'll tackle **Migrating an Existing Codebase** to replace ad-hoc components with your unified design-system library.

7.2 Migrating an Existing Codebase to the Design System

Goal Statement
In this section you'll learn how to incrementally replace legacy UI code—ad-hoc components, inline styles, and hard-coded values—with your centralized design-system library, ensuring minimal disruption and maximal safety during the transition.

Key Terms

- **Strangler Pattern**
- **Incremental Migration**
- **Alias Mapping**
- **Deprecation**
- **Code Modularity**

Practical Outcome
By the end, you'll have a strategy to swap out legacy buttons, inputs, and layouts for your design-system equivalents one screen or feature at a time, maintain backwards compatibility, and track deprecations until the old code can be safely removed.

Research & Gather Notes

- **Official Docs & Blogs**
    - Martin Fowler's "Strangler Fig" pattern for gradual system replacement.
    - Articles on migration strategies in large React codebases.
- **Community Examples**
    - GitHub: Migrating from Bootstrap to a custom component library.
    - Blog: "How we migrated 100k lines of CSS into Storybook-driven design system."
- **Your Own Experience**
    - Found that adding aliases (`import { Button } from 'ui/Button'`) helps you swap implementations without touching imports.
    - Learned to use lint-rules to flag legacy component usage and guard new code.

Rewriting an entire application in one go is risky and costly. Instead, apply the **strangler** approach: surround the old system with the new design system, gradually routing new UI to the library while phasing out legacy code. Begin by installing your design-system package into the existing repo, then systematically replace ad-hoc components (buttons, inputs, cards) with their design-system equivalents on a per-screen or per-feature basis.

Use **module aliasing** (e.g. `import { Button } from '@your-org/design-system';`) alongside your current imports so you can flip a switch in your build config to point `ui/Button` to either the old or new implementation. Maintain both in parallel: deprecate the legacy components via eslint warnings, update each usage to the new library, then remove the old code once all usages are migrated.

Concept Breakdown

1. **Strangler Pattern**
   - Incrementally replace functionality by routing traffic to new code around the old.
2. **Alias Mapping**
   - Use `webpack` or `tsconfig` aliases so imports can point to either implementation based on migration progress.
3. **Deprecation Warnings**
   - Lint rules or console warnings flag usage of deprecated components to guide developers.
4. **Feature-by-Feature Migration**
   - Tackle one UI area at a time (e.g., header, forms, dashboard) to keep PRs small and reviewable.
5. **Automated Tests**
   - Update or add snapshot and visual regression tests for both old and new until migration completes.

---

4. Code Walkthrough

```
// tsconfig.json: configure alias for UI components
{
  "compilerOptions": {
    "baseUrl": ".",
    "paths": {
      "ui/Button": ["src/legacy/Button.jsx"],
// old until migrated
      // once migrated, switch to:
      // "ui/Button": ["node_modules/@your-org/design-
system/Button"]
    }
  }
}
// .eslintrc.js: deprecation rule
module.exports = {
  rules: {
    "no-restricted-imports": [
      "warn",
      {
        "paths": [
          {
            "name": "src/legacy/Button.jsx",
```

```
            "message": "Please use `@your-org/design-system`
Button instead."
          }
        ]
      }
    ]
  }
};
// src/components/Profile.jsx (before)
import LegacyButton from 'ui/Button';
...
<LegacyButton onClick={save}>Save</LegacyButton>
// after alias switch and import rename
import { Button } from '@your-org/design-system';
...
<Button onClick={save}>Save</Button>
```

- **What it does:**
  - Uses a path alias to abstract the source of the component.
  - Lints against legacy imports, prompting developers to adopt the design system.
  - Swapping the alias in your config migrates all imports at once.
- **Why this approach:**
  - **Low risk:** You control the cut-over point.
  - **Developer guidance:** Warnings steer code toward the new components.
  - **Incremental:** You can migrate one screen or module per sprint.

Common Pitfalls

1. **Alias Inconsistency**
   - Forgetting to update both webpack and IDE configs leads to broken imports.
   - **Fix:** Mirror your alias in `tsconfig.json`, Webpack, and ESLint.
2. **Untracked Legacy Uses**
   - Some developers may still import directly from legacy paths.
   - **Fix:** Enforce restricted-imports lint rule and run a codemod to rewrite imports.
3. **CSS Conflicts**
   - Legacy styles may clash with design-system CSS variables.

- Fix: Isolate legacy components in a CSS namespace or remove global CSS gradually.

Migration Strangler Switch

```
┌──────────────────────────────┐
│ import 'ui/Button'           │
└──────────────────────────────┘
              │ alias config
              ▼
┌──────────────────────────────┐
│  v1 → src/legacy/Button      │   (legacy)
│  v2 → @design-system         │   (new)
└──────────────────────────────┘
```

Hands-On Exercise

Objective: Begin migrating one feature to your design system.

1. **Configure Aliases:**
   - Add path mapping for `ui/Button`, `ui/TextInput`, and `ui/Container` in your `tsconfig.json` (or Webpack).
2. **Set Up ESLint Warnings:**
   - Add `no-restricted-imports` rules to warn when importing `src/legacy/*` directly.
3. **Migrate a Screen:**
   - Choose a simple page (e.g., login form).
   - Replace legacy `Button`, `Input`, and layout with design-system versions, updating imports.
4. **Verify Compatibility:**
   - Run the app, ensure styling and behavior remain correct.
   - Confirm ESLint warnings for any remaining legacy imports.
5. **Deliverable:**
   - Updated alias config and ESLint rules.
   - A pull request showing replaced imports and no styling regressions on the migrated screen.

Key Takeaways

- Use the **strangler pattern** and path aliases to swap implementations with minimal code churn.
- Enforce deprecation via lint rules and codemods to guide the team.
- Migrate feature by feature, verifying styling and tests at each step.

Next Steps
Proceed to **Section 7.3**, where we'll explore **Managing Monorepos with Lerna or Nx**—scaling your design-system across multiple packages and applications within a single repository.

7.3 Managing Monorepos with Lerna or Nx

Goal Statement
In this section you'll learn how to structure and manage a monorepo for your design-system, applications, and shared packages using tools like **Lerna** or **Nx**—enabling synchronized versioning, streamlined dependency management, and consistent builds across multiple projects.

Key Terms

- **Monorepo**
- **Lerna**
- **Nx**
- **Workspaces**
- **Task Orchestration**

Practical Outcome
By the end, you'll be able to set up a monorepo with your design-system and a consumer app as separate packages, configure shared dependencies, run cross-package builds/tests, and publish versioned packages in lockstep.

Research & Gather Notes

- **Official Docs & Blogs**
  - Lerna "Getting Started" guide.
  - Nx "Monorepo" documentation.

- **Community Examples**
    - GitHub: `nx create-nx-workspace` for React + library.
    - GitHub: Lerna-managed monorepos for component libraries and docs sites.
- **Your Own Experience**
    - Found Nx's built-in task graph and caching speeds up CI significantly.
    - Learned Lerna's versioning modes (fixed vs. independent) and when to use each.

A **monorepo** houses multiple related packages—your design-system, demo app, internal utilities—in a single repository. **Lerna** and **Nx** both provide tooling to manage versioning, dependencies, and task execution across packages. Lerna excels at simple package grouping and synchronized releases; Nx adds powerful dependency graphs, caching, and advanced generators. Choosing the right tool helps teams collaborate, share code, and maintain consistency without sacrificing performance.

Concept Breakdown

1. **Monorepo**
    - Single Git repo containing multiple `package.json` workspaces under a common root.
2. **Lerna**
    - Manages multiple npm packages, with commands for bootstrap, link, version, and publish.
    - **Fixed mode:** all packages share one version.
    - **Independent mode:** each package can version separately.
3. **Nx**
    - Provides workspace generators, affected-graph build/test, distributed caching, and built-in lint/test/serve executors.
    - Encourages a "project graph" approach for incremental CI.
4. **Workspaces**
    - Yarn or npm workspaces link local packages together and hoist common dependencies to the root.
5. **Task Orchestration**
    - Running scripts (build, test, lint) across multiple packages efficiently, skipping unaffected projects.

---

4. Code Walkthrough

A. Lerna Setup (Fixed Mode)

```
# 1. Initialize
npx lerna init

# 2. Update lerna.json
# {
#   "packages": ["packages/*"],
#   "version": "0.1.0"
# }

# 3. Bootstrap dependencies
npx lerna bootstrap

# 4. Add packages
mkdir -p packages/design-system packages/consumer-app
# each with its own package.json and src/

# 5. Publish
npx lerna publish from-git
```

B. Nx Setup

```
# 1. Create workspace
npx create-nx-workspace@latest my-monorepo --preset=empty

# 2. Generate libraries/apps
nx g @nrwl/react:library design-system --directory=packages
nx g @nrwl/react:application consumer-app --
directory=packages

# 3. Install dependencies
npm install

# 4. Run tasks
nx build design-system
nx serve consumer-app
nx test design-system
```

- **What it does:**
  - **Lerna:** links packages, hoists deps, and versions them together.
  - **Nx:** scaffolds apps/libs, tracks dependencies, and optimizes task runs via caching.
- **Why this approach:**
  - **Consistency:** Single repo for all related code.

- **Efficiency:** Shared node_modules, parallel task execution, and caching reduce CI time.

Common Pitfalls

1. **Dependency Hoisting Conflicts**
   - Hoisted packages can lead to mismatched versions.
   - **Fix:** Pin versions in root `package.json` and use `nohoist` for exceptions.
2. **Slow CI on Large Repos**
   - Building all packages every time is inefficient.
   - **Fix:** Use Nx's affected commands (`nx affected:build`) or Lerna's `--since` flag.
3. **Inconsistent Versioning**
   - Independent mode can lead to version drift across related packages.
   - **Fix:** Choose fixed mode for libraries that should version in tandem.

```
Monorepo Structure

my-monorepo/
├── package.json         (root workspaces)
├── lerna.json / nx.json
├── packages/
│   ├── design-system/
│   │   ├ package.json
│   │   └ src/
│   └── consumer-app/
│       ├ package.json
│       └ src/
└── node_modules/
```

Hands-On Exercise

Objective: Convert your projects into a monorepo with Lerna or Nx.

1. **Choose Tool:**
   - Decide between Lerna (simplicity) or Nx (advanced caching).
2. **Initialize:**
   - Run `npx lerna init` or `npx create-nx-workspace`.

3. **Organize Packages:**
    - Move your `design-system` and `consumer-app` into `packages/`.
4. **Bootstrap & Test:**
    - Link dependencies (`lerna bootstrap` or `npm install` + `nx run-many`).
    - Build and run both projects (`nx build`, `nx serve` or `lerna run build --stream`).
5. **Deliverable:**
    - A working monorepo where `npm run build` builds all packages, and `nx affected:build` or `lerna run build --since` builds only changed ones.

Key Takeaways

- **Monorepos** centralize multiple packages in one repository for easier sharing and consistency.
- **Lerna** provides straightforward package linking and synchronized versioning.
- **Nx** offers powerful task orchestration, caching, and generators for large-scale monorepos.

Next Steps
Proceed to **Section 7.4**, where we'll set up **Continuous Integration and Automated Releases** across your monorepo—ensuring every package is tested, built, and published efficiently.

7.4 Continuous Integration and Automated Releases

Goal Statement
In this section you'll learn how to configure a **Continuous Integration (CI)** pipeline that automatically builds, tests, and publishes your monorepo's packages—and ties into your automated release workflow so that every merge to `main` triggers new releases of your design-system and apps.

Key Terms

- **CI Pipeline**

- **GitHub Actions / GitLab CI / CircleCI**
- **Build & Test Jobs**
- **Release Workflow**
- **Artifact Publishing**

Practical Outcome
By the end, you'll have a CI configuration that runs lint/build/test across all packages, conditionally publishes changed packages to npm (via semantic-release or Lerna), and generates GitHub Releases or Docker images—ensuring reliable, hands-off deployments.

Research & Gather Notes

- **Official Docs & Blogs**
  - GitHub Actions "CI for monorepos" best practices.
  - Semantic-release "CI configuration" guide.
- **Community Examples**
  - GitHub: Lerna + GitHub Actions workflow for building and releasing multiple packages.
  - GitLab CI examples for Nx monorepos.
- **Your Own Experience**
  - Found that splitting jobs by task (lint, test, build, release) and leveraging caching greatly speeds up CI.
  - Learned to use conditionals so only changed packages are released, avoiding unnecessary publishes.

A robust CI pipeline enforces code quality and automates deployment. For a monorepo, CI should run **lint**, **unit tests**, and **build** for all or only affected packages. Upon passing, your CI should trigger the release process—bumping versions, generating changelogs, and publishing updated packages to npm or Docker registries. We'll demonstrate a GitHub Actions workflow that orchestrates these steps, integrates with semantic-release (or Lerna), and uses caching to optimize performance.

Concept Breakdown

1. **Lint / Test / Build Jobs**
   - Separate jobs for clarity: `lint`, `test`, `build`.
   - Use matrix or affected-graph to limit to changed packages.

2. **Caching Dependencies**
   - Cache `~/.npm` or `node_modules` between runs to speed up installs.
   - Cache build outputs or Nx's computation cache.
3. **Conditional Releases**
   - Only publish packages with relevant changes—via `semantic-release`'s analysis or `lerna changed`.
4. **Secrets Management**
   - Store `NPM_TOKEN`, `GITHUB_TOKEN`, and any registry credentials in CI secrets.
5. **Artifact Publishing**
   - Optionally upload build artifacts (e.g. storybook, coverage reports) as CI artifacts or deploy to hosting.

---

4. Code Walkthrough

```
# .github/workflows/ci.yml
name: CI & Release

on:
  push:
    branches: [ main ]
  pull_request:
    branches: [ '*' ]

jobs:
  lint:
    runs-on: ubuntu-latest
    steps:
      - uses: actions/checkout@v3
      - uses: actions/setup-node@v3
        with: node-version: '18'
      - run: npm ci
      - run: npm run lint

  test:
    needs: lint
    runs-on: ubuntu-latest
    steps:
      - uses: actions/checkout@v3
      - uses: actions/setup-node@v3
        with: node-version: '18'
      - run: npm ci
      - run: npm test -- --ci
```

```yaml
build:
  needs: test
  runs-on: ubuntu-latest
  steps:
    - uses: actions/checkout@v3
    - uses: actions/setup-node@v3
      with: node-version: '18'
    - run: npm ci
    - run: npm run build --workspaces

release:
  needs: build
  if: github.ref == 'refs/heads/main'
  runs-on: ubuntu-latest
  steps:
    - uses: actions/checkout@v3
    - uses: actions/setup-node@v3
      with:
        node-version: '18'
        registry-url: 'https://registry.npmjs.org/'
    - run: npm ci
    - name: Semantic Release
      env:
        NPM_TOKEN: ${{ secrets.NPM_TOKEN }}
        GITHUB_TOKEN: ${{ secrets.GITHUB_TOKEN }}
      run: npx semantic-release
```

- **What it does:**
  - **lint/test/build**: sequentially ensures code quality and successful builds.
  - **release**: on `main` branch, runs `semantic-release` to detect changed packages, bump versions, generate changelog, and publish.
- **Why this approach:**
  - **Reliability:** Each step gates the next, preventing broken code from releasing.
  - **Efficiency:** Caching and workspace flags speed monorepo tasks.
  - **Automation:** Fully hands-off releases driven by commit history and CI.

Common Pitfalls

1. **Token Misconfiguration**

   - Missing or incorrect `NPM_TOKEN` prevents publishing.
   - **Fix:** Verify tokens in repo settings and test with a dry run.
2. **CI Timeouts**
   - Long builds can exceed time limits.
   - **Fix:** Use caching, split jobs, or increase timeout settings.
3. **Unintended Releases**
   - Publishing on every push, not just versioned commits.
   - **Fix:** Ensure `semantic-release` only runs on `main` and uses proper commit conventions.

```
CI & Release Workflow

Push to main
      |
┌─────▼─────┐
|   lint    |
└─────┬─────┘
      |
┌─────▼─────┐
|   test    |
└─────┬─────┘
      |
┌─────▼─────┐
|   build   |
└─────┬─────┘
      |
┌─────▼─────┐
|release (semantic-release)|
└─────────────────────────┘
```

Hands-On Exercise

Objective: Implement CI & automated releases for your monorepo.

1. **Add CI Workflow:**
   - Create `.github/workflows/ci.yml` as above.
2. **Configure Secrets:**
   - Add `NPM_TOKEN` and `GITHUB_TOKEN` to GitHub repo secrets.
3. **Test Pipeline:**
   - Push a `feat:` commit to `main`, verify lint/test/build pass and a new release is published.
4. **Validate Artifacts:**
   - Confirm new package version on npm and release notes on GitHub.

Key Takeaways

- A CI pipeline with lint, test, build, and release jobs ensures quality and automates deployment.
- **Semantic-release** leverages commit history to version and publish packages without manual intervention.
- Proper caching, workspace flags, and secrets management make CI fast, reliable, and secure.

Next Steps
Proceed to **Chapter 8**, where we'll cover **Collaboration, Governance, and Scaling**—defining contribution guidelines, code-review workflows, and governance processes to support growing teams using your design system.

Visual Aid: CI/CD Pipeline Diagram (ASCII)

```
CI/CD Pipeline Diagram

     [Developer Push]
             │
             ▼
     ┌─────────────────┐
     │    Checkout     │
     │ actions/checkout │
     └────────┬────────┘
             │
             ▼
     ┌─────────────────┐
     │  Install Deps   │
     │   npm ci        │
     └────────┬────────┘
             │
             ▼
     ┌─────────────────┐
     │      Lint       │
     │ npm run lint    │
     └────────┬────────┘
             │
             ▼
     ┌─────────────────┐
     │      Test       │
```

```
│ npm test --ci │
└───────┬───────┘
        │
        ▼
┌───────────────┐
│     Build     │
│ npm run build │
└───────┬───────┘
        │
        ▼
┌──────────────────────────┐
│ Conditional Release Job  │
│ (on main branch only)    │
│ npm run semantic-release │
└───────┬──────────────────┘
        │
        ▼
┌───────────────┐
│  Publish to   │
│ npm & GitHub  │
└───────────────┘
```

7.5 End-of-Chapter Summary & Key Takeaways

1. **Consuming in Create React App**
   - Install your published `@your-org/design-system` package (plus any peer dependencies) via npm or Yarn.
   - Import the library's global CSS (tokens, resets) in `src/index.js` and wrap your app in the `<ThemeProvider>`.
   - Verify that atoms, molecules, and layout primitives render correctly in the new CRA.
2. **Migrating an Existing Codebase**
   - Apply the **strangler pattern**: incrementally replace legacy UI with design-system components.
   - Use path aliases (`ui/Button`) and ESLint deprecation rules to guide developers toward the new library.
   - Migrate feature-by-feature, verifying styling and behavior remain consistent.
3. **Managing a Monorepo with Lerna or Nx**
   - Structure your repo into separate packages (e.g. `packages/design-system`, `packages/consumer-app`).
   - Leverage workspaces for dependency hoisting and linkage, and choose between Lerna's simple bootstrap/versioning or Nx's task graph, generators, and caching.

    - Run cross-package builds, tests, and serves via workspace scripts or Nx commands.
4. **Continuous Integration & Automated Releases**
    - Configure a CI workflow (e.g., GitHub Actions) with sequential jobs: lint → test → build → release.
    - Integrate **semantic-release** (or Lerna) to automatically bump versions, generate `CHANGELOG.md`, and publish packages on merges to `main`.
    - Use caching and workspace flags to optimize install and build times, and guard releases with proper secret management.

— With your design system consumed, migrated, monorepo-managed, and CI/CD-enabled, you're ready to establish processes for collaboration and governance at scale in **Chapter 8**.

7.6 Hands-On Exercises

Exercise 1: Consume Your Design System in a Fresh CRA

- **Objective:** Verify seamless integration of your published library.
- **Steps:**
    1. Create a new CRA project:
    2. `npx create-react-app my-consumer-app`
    3. `cd my-consumer-app`
    4. Install your design system and any peer deps:
    5. `npm install @your-org/design-system styled-components`
    6. In `src/index.js`, import the global CSS and wrap <App> with <ThemeProvider> from your library.
    7. In `src/App.js`, render a <Container>, a <TextInput>, and a <Button> from your design system.
    8. Run `npm start` and confirm all components render with correct styles.
- **Deliverable:**
    - Screenshot of the running app with your components.
    - Console verification of no peer-dependency warnings.

Exercise 2: Incremental Migration of a Legacy Screen

- **Objective:** Apply the strangler pattern to replace legacy components.
- **Steps:**
    1. In an existing React repo, configure a path alias `ui/Button` pointing initially to `src/legacy/Button.jsx`.
    2. Add an ESLint rule warning when importing `src/legacy`, guiding developers to `@your-org/design-system`.
    3. Identify a simple screen (e.g., a login form) using legacy `<Button>` and `<Input>`.
    4. Update imports to `import { Button, TextInput } from '@your-org/design-system';`.
    5. Flip the alias to point `ui/Button` at your design-system's `<Button>`, rebuild, and verify no style regressions.
- **Deliverable:**
    - Diff showing alias config change and updated imports.
    - Before/after screenshots of the screen.

Exercise 3: Set Up a Monorepo with Your Library and App

- **Objective:** Manage your packages together in one repo.
- **Steps (choose Lerna or Nx):**
    - **Lerna**:
        1. Run `npx lerna init` and move your `design-system` and `consumer-app` into `packages/`.
        2. Configure `lerna.json` with `"packages": ["packages/*"]`.
        3. Run `npx lerna bootstrap`, then `npx lerna run build --stream`.
    - **Nx**:
        1. Run `npx create-nx-workspace@latest repo --preset=empty`.
        2. Generate `design-system` library and `consumer-app` application under `packages/`.
        3. Run `nx build design-system` and `nx serve consumer-app`.
- **Deliverable:**
    - Repo file tree showing `packages/` structure.

    - Log output of successful bootstrap/build/serve commands.

Exercise 4: Implement CI & Automated Releases

- **Objective:** Ensure every commit is tested, built, and released automatically.
- **Steps:**
    1. Add `.github/workflows/ci.yml` with jobs for **lint**, **test**, **build**, and **release** (using `semantic-release`).
    2. Store `NPM_TOKEN` and `GITHUB_TOKEN` in GitHub secrets.
    3. Push a `fix:` commit to `main` and observe the CI pipeline: lint → test → build → release.
    4. Confirm on npm and GitHub that a new patch version is published with updated changelog.
- **Deliverable:**
    - Screenshot of GitHub Actions workflow passing.
    - Link to the newly published package version and its release notes on GitHub.

7.7 Next Steps: Setting Up GitHub Actions

Goal Statement
In this section you'll configure GitHub Actions workflows to automate your monorepo's CI/CD—from linting and testing through building and releasing—so every push and pull request is validated and merged code is deployed without manual intervention.

Key Terms

- **Workflow**
- **Job**
- **Runner**
- **Matrix Strategy**
- **Secrets**

Practical Outcome
By the end, you'll have a `.github/workflows/ci.yml` that runs your lint, test, and build jobs, plus a `.github/workflows/release.yml` that invokes

your release tool (e.g. `semantic-release` or `lerna publish`) whenever code lands on `main`.

---

2. Explanatory Text

Automating your pipeline with GitHub Actions ensures consistency and frees you from one-off scripts. A **workflow** file describes triggers (such as `push` or `pull_request`), and one or more **jobs** run on virtual **runners**. You can use a **matrix** to test against multiple Node versions or OSes, and store credentials like `NPM_TOKEN` and `GITHUB_TOKEN` in repository **secrets**.

A typical setup splits concerns:

- **ci.yml**
  - Triggered on `pull_request` and on `push` to feature branches.
  - Jobs:
    1. Checkout & setup Node
    2. Install dependencies (`npm ci`)
    3. Run `npm run lint`
    4. Run `npm test --ci`
    5. Run `npm run build --workspaces`
- **release.yml**
  - Triggered on `push` to `main`.
  - Jobs:
    1. Checkout & setup Node with registry auth
    2. Install dependencies
    3. Run `npx semantic-release` (or `npx lerna publish --yes`)

By separating CI from release, you ensure that only code that passes all checks is promoted to a published package.

---

3. Code Walkthrough

```
# .github/workflows/ci.yml
name: CI

on:
```

```
  pull_request:
    branches: [ '**' ]
  push:
    branches-ignore: [ main ]

jobs:
  lint-test-build:
    runs-on: ubuntu-latest
    strategy:
      matrix:
        node-version: [16, 18]
    steps:
      - uses: actions/checkout@v3
      - uses: actions/setup-node@v3
        with:
          node-version: ${{ matrix['node-version'] }}
      - name: Install dependencies
        run: npm ci
      - name: Lint
        run: npm run lint
      - name: Test
        run: npm test -- --ci
      - name: Build
        run: npm run build --workspaces
# .github/workflows/release.yml
name: Release

on:
  push:
    branches: [ main ]

jobs:
  release:
    runs-on: ubuntu-latest
    steps:
      - uses: actions/checkout@v3
      - uses: actions/setup-node@v3
        with:
          node-version: '18'
          registry-url: 'https://registry.npmjs.org/'
      - name: Install dependencies
        run: npm ci
      - name: Publish Packages
        env:
          NPM_TOKEN: ${{ secrets.NPM_TOKEN }}
          GITHUB_TOKEN: ${{ secrets.GITHUB_TOKEN }}
        run: npx semantic-release
```

---

4. Common Pitfalls

1. **Missing Secrets**
   - Workflows that publish require tokens stored under **Settings > Secrets**.
2. **Overlapping Triggers**
   - Be sure your CI workflow does **not** run release steps on feature branches.
3. **Long-Running Jobs**
   - Split heavy steps (build vs. test) into separate jobs and leverage caching for speed.

End-of-Section Summary & Next Steps

Key Takeaways

- Use **ci.yml** to validate PRs: lint, test, build.
- Use **release.yml** on `main` to publish your library automatically.
- Store your credentials securely and use a matrix strategy to test across Node versions.

Next Steps
With GitHub Actions in place, your design system is validated and deployed automatically. In **Chapter 8**, we'll define **Collaboration, Governance, and Scaling** practices—establishing contribution guidelines, review workflows, and governance models to support a growing user base.

Chapter 8: Collaboration, Governance, and Scaling

8.1 Establishing Contribution Guidelines

Goal Statement
In this section you'll learn how to create clear, concise contribution guidelines—including coding standards, branch/commit conventions, and PR workflows—so that new and existing contributors can onboard quickly and maintain consistent quality across your design system.

Key Terms

- **CONTRIBUTING.md**
- **Code of Conduct**
- **Issue & PR Templates**
- **Conventional Commits**
- **Branch Naming**

Practical Outcome
By the end, you'll publish a `CONTRIBUTING.md` at your repo root, define GitHub issue and pull-request templates, enforce Conventional Commits via a commit-lint hook, and outline your review and merge criteria—providing a single source of truth for all contributions.

Why Contribution Guidelines Matter

Without documented guidelines, contributors waste time guessing your workflow—resulting in disparate commit styles, inconsistent PRs, and stalled reviews. A well-structured CONTRIBUTING.md:

- Sets clear expectations for reporting bugs and requesting features
- Standardizes branch names (e.g. `feature/…`, `fix/…`) and commit messages (`feat:`, `fix:`, `docs:`)
- Provides step-by-step setup instructions, reducing environment issues
- Embeds templates to capture necessary context in issues and PRs
- Details your review process (number of approvals, required checks)

Key Components of Your CONTRIBUTING.md

1. **Introduction & Thank You**
   - A friendly welcome and quick "thank you" to contributors.
2. **Code of Conduct**
   - Link to or embed your CoC, ensuring an inclusive environment.
3. **Getting Started**

```
git clone git@github.com:your-org/design-system.git
cd design-system
npm ci
npm run bootstrap     # link workspaces
npm run dev           # start Storybook
```

4. **Branching & Commits**
   - **Branch names:** `feature/your-feature`, `fix/your-bug`
   - **Commits:** Follow Conventional Commits:
   - `feat(button): add outline variant`
   - `fix(modal): correct focus trap`
   - `docs: update changelog for v1.2.0`
   - Enforce via commit-lint & Husky pre-commit hook.
5. **Issue Templates**
   - Create `.github/ISSUE_TEMPLATE/bug_report.md` and `feature_request.md` prompting reproduction steps, expected behavior, and screenshots.
6. **Pull Request Process**
   - Use `.github/PULL_REQUEST_TEMPLATE.md` with a checklist:
     - Code follows lint rules
     - Tests added/updated
     - Storybook stories included
     - Change documented in CHANGELOG.md
     - Visual diffs reviewed (Chromatic)
7. **Review & Merge Criteria**
   - Require passing CI (lint, tests, a11y, visual)
   - At least one developer and one designer approval for visual changes
   - Merge with "Squash and merge" to keep history clean
8. **Additional Resources**
   - Link to CONTRIBUTING.md, CODE_OF_CONDUCT.md, and developer setup docs.

Hands-On Exercise

1. **Draft CONTRIBUTING.md**
   - Include all sections above in your repository root.
2. **Add Templates**
   - Under `.github/ISSUE_TEMPLATE/`, add `bug_report.md` and `feature_request.md`.
   - Add `.github/PULL_REQUEST_TEMPLATE.md` with the review checklist.
3. **Enforce Conventions**
   - Install `@commitlint/config-conventional` and configure Husky to run commit-lint.
   - Ensure your CI workflow fails on lint or test errors for PRs.
4. **Verify**
   - Open a test issue and PR to see templates in action.
   - Commit with an invalid message to confirm commit-lint blocks it.

End-of-Section Summary

- A **CONTRIBUTING.md** centralizes all on-boarding instructions, conventions, and workflows.
- **Templates** for issues and PRs ensure contributors provide complete information upfront.
- **Automated checks** (commit-lint, CI) enforce consistency and quality.
- Clear **review criteria** expedite merges and maintain high standards.

8.2 Code Reviews and Visual QA Workflows

Goal Statement
In this section you'll learn how to establish rigorous code-review practices and integrate visual QA checks—leveraging automated tools and human sign-off—to ensure each pull request maintains functional correctness, accessibility, and visual consistency.

Key Terms

- **Pull Request (PR) Review**
- **Review Checklist**
- **Automated Lint & Tests**
- **Visual Regression**
- **Designer Sign-Off**

Practical Outcome
By the end, you'll have a standardized PR review process—including automated pipelines for linting, unit tests, a11y scans, visual diff reports—and a lightweight manual acceptance step for designers to approve UX and visual changes before merge.

Research & Gather Notes

- **Official Docs & Blogs**
  - GitHub's "About pull request reviews" documentation.
  - Storybook's guidance on using Chromatic for visual review.
- **Community Examples**
  - Atlassian's PR templates requiring screenshots and test results.
  - Microsoft's Fluent UI PR process combining code and design reviews.
- **Your Own Experience**
  - Noted that combining automated a11y checks and visual diffs catches most regressions; designers then focus only on subjective styling.
  - Learned that a simple checklist in the PR description keeps reviewers aligned.

A robust review process balances automation with human oversight. **Automated checks**—lint, unit/integration tests, `@axe-core` a11y scans, and visual snapshot comparisons—catch regressions early and free reviewers from mundane checks. **Human reviewers** then focus on architecture, API design, and user experience nuances. Finally, a **visual QA step**, typically via Chromatic or Percy, surfaces pixel-level diffs for designers to approve, ensuring the library's look and feel remains intentional.

We'll define a **PR review checklist** for engineers and a lightweight **design-approval workflow** that integrates with your CI's visual-diff tool. This dual-track approach scales: developers enforce technical correctness and accessibility, while designers verify visual polish only when changes exceed a threshold.

Concept Breakdown

1. **Automated Checks**
   - **Lint & Types:** `npm run lint` and `tsc --noEmit` for code consistency.
   - **Unit/Integration Tests:** `npm test --ci` to validate behavior.
   - **Accessibility Scans:** `@axe-core/react` logs and fails on critical violations.
   - **Visual Regression:** Chromatic job flags diffs on component stories.
2. **PR Review Checklist**
   - Ensure all automated checks pass.
   - Confirm new components include stories and docs.
   - Verify commit messages follow Conventional Commits.
   - Check that token usage and theming are consistent.
3. **Designer Sign-Off**
   - Designers review visual diff report links from Chromatic.
   - Approve or comment on UI changes before merge.
4. **GitHub Labels & Templates**
   - Use labels like `needs-dev-review`, `needs-design-review`, `visual-diff`.
   - PR template prompts author to upload manual screenshots for complex visual changes.
5. **Merge Conditions**
   - Require `status: passing` for lint/test/a11y/visual checks.
   - Enforce at least one developer and one designer approval on PR.

Code Review & QA Workflow Example

```
### Pull Request Checklist

- [ ] Code builds locally (`npm run build`)
- [ ] Linting & type checks passed
- [ ] All unit/integration tests passing
- [ ] No critical a11y violations (`@axe-core/react`)
```

```
- [ ] Storybook stories added/updated
- [ ] Chromatic visual diffs reviewed:
    - [ ] Approved by designer
- [ ] Commit messages follow Conventional Commits
- [ ] Documentation updated (CHANGELOG, CONTRIBUTING, MDX)
# Relevant CI job annotations
jobs:
  lint:
    # runs lint & type-check
  test:
    # runs tests & a11y scans
  chromatic:
    # runs visual regression, requires label `visual-diff`
```

- **What it does:**
  - Automates guardrails against technical regressions.
  - Guides developers through a clear checklist.
  - Involves designers only when visual changes occur.
- **Why this approach:**
  - **Efficiency:** Automation frees reviewers to focus on strategic feedback.
  - **Quality:** Multiple layers of checks catch different classes of issues.
  - **Collaboration:** Clear roles for developers and designers reduce friction.

Common Pitfalls

1. **Ignoring Visual Diffs**
   - Merging PRs without reviewing reported diffs leads to unintended visual bugs.
   - **Fix:** Enforce a required `visual-diff` status check and designer approval label.
2. **Checklist Fatigue**
   - Overly long PR checklists become noise.
   - **Fix:** Keep the checklist concise; automate as many items as possible.
3. **Late Discovery of A11y Issues**
   - Running accessibility scans only on staging misses early fixes.
   - **Fix:** Integrate `@axe-core/react` in dev and as a CI job on every PR.

Hands-On Exercise

Objective: Implement a combined developer and design review workflow.

1. **PR Template:**
   - Create `.github/PULL_REQUEST_TEMPLATE.md` with the above checklist and label reminders.
2. **CI Integration:**
   - Ensure your GitHub Actions `ci.yml` includes a job for `npx axe` or similar a11y tool.
   - Verify your visual-regression workflow (Chromatic) reports a status check named `visual-diff`.
3. **Branch Protection:**
   - Configure GitHub branch rules requiring passing checks for `lint`, `test`, `visual-diff`, and approvals from both developer and designer teams.
4. **Mock PR:**
   - Submit a test PR that tweaks a component's color or spacing.
   - Observe automated failures (if any), fix issues, and route the visual-diff to a designer for sign-off.
5. **Deliverable:**
   - PR URL illustrating the workflow: automated checks, checklist in description, labels, and designer-approved visual diff.

Key Takeaways

- Combine **automated checks** (lint/test/a11y/visual) with a **human review** checklist to maintain high quality.
- Use **PR templates** and **labels** to guide contributors and reviewers.
- Enforce **branch protection** so no PR can merge without passing all checks and obtaining necessary approvals.

Next Steps
Proceed to **Section 8.3**, where we'll define **Cross-Functional Design-Dev Hand-Offs**—streamlining how designers and developers collaborate on new components, from Figma to code.

8.3 Cross-Functional Design-Dev Hand-Offs

Goal Statement
In this section you'll learn how to streamline collaboration between designers and developers—establishing shared tooling, communication channels, and processes—to translate design assets into code efficiently and accurately.

Key Terms

- **Design Tokens**
- **Figma Components**
- **Code Snippets / Auto-Generated CSS**
- **Inspect Mode**
- **Versioned Libraries**

Practical Outcome
By the end, you'll have a hand-off workflow where designers publish a versioned component library in Figma, developers pull matching design tokens or code snippets, and both sides sync updates via a shared registry—minimizing misunderstandings and rework.

Research & Gather Notes

- **Official Docs & Blogs**
  - Figma's "Design System Analytics" and Team Libraries guide.
  - UXPin's article on design–dev collaboration.
- **Community Examples**
  - GitHub: "Figma Tokens" plugin workflows that export JSON tokens.
  - Blog: "Bridging the gap between Figma and React" using style-dictionary.
- **Your Own Experience**
  - Found that automating token export from Figma reduces drift between design and code.
  - Learned that a shared Slack or Teams channel tagged for "design-dev" accelerates quick clarifications.

Effective hand-off is not a one-time event but an ongoing sync between design and development. When designers update colors, spacing, or component layouts, developers need an immediate, machine-readable way to consume those changes. Conversely, developers may need to request clarifications or adjustments. A robust process uses:

1. **Versioned Design Libraries**
   - Designers publish reusable Figma components and tokens as a team library, each version tagged (e.g., v1.2).
2. **Automated Token Exports**
   - Use plugins (e.g., Figma Tokens, Style Dictionary) to export design tokens (colors, typography, spacing) as JSON or CSS variables.
3. **Shared Registry**
   - Store exported token artifacts in a package registry or Git repo; developers install or pull updates via CI.
4. **Inspect Mode & Code Snippets**
   - Designers enable Figma's Inspect panel so devs can copy CSS properties, SVG paths, and layout details directly.
5. **Feedback Loop**
   - A dedicated Slack channel or ticketing label (e.g., `design-dev-handoff`) ensures questions and change requests are tracked.

This continuous integration of design assets into code prevents drift, accelerates iterations, and empowers both teams to focus on their strengths.

Workflow Example

```
flowchart LR
  A[Designer updates Figma tokens] --> B[Figma Tokens plugin
exports JSON]
  B --> C[Commit token JSON to tokens-repo]
  C --> D[CI publishes tokens@version to npm/private
registry]
  D --> E[Developer installs or updates @design-system-
tokens]
  E --> F[Build regenerates CSS variables and TS types]
  F --> G[App reflects new design values]
  G --> H[QA verifies visual fidelity]
  H --> A[Feedback to designer if discrepancies]
```

Common Pitfalls

1. **Manual Copy-Paste of Styles**
   - Leads to outdated values; avoid by automating token exports.
2. **Version Mismatch**
   - Devs using old token versions cause inconsistent UI; enforce semantic versioning for design libraries.
3. **Lack of Communication Channel**
   - Design questions get lost in general chat; create a dedicated `#design-dev` channel or label.

Hands-On Exercise

Objective: Establish an end-to-end design–dev hand-off for your color and spacing tokens.

1. **Publish Figma Library:**
   - In Figma, create a Team Library for colors and spacing tokens; tag a release (e.g., "v1.0").
2. **Export Tokens:**
   - Install the Figma Tokens plugin and export your tokens as JSON.
   - Commit the JSON to a `design-tokens` repo under `tokens/v1.0.json`.
3. **Automate Publication:**
   - Set up a GitHub Action in the `design-tokens` repo that, on push to main, publishes the JSON as an npm package `@your-org/design-tokens@<version>`.
4. **Consume in Code:**
   - In your design-system codebase, add `@your-org/design-tokens` as a dependency.
   - Create a build step that reads the JSON and generates CSS variables and TypeScript types (e.g., via Style Dictionary).
5. **Verify:**
   - Update a color in Figma, bump the library version, export, and publish.
   - In your app, update token version, rebuild, and confirm the new color appears in the UI.

Summary

- **Versioned Libraries** in Figma ensure designers and developers target the same component set.
- **Automated Token Exports** bridge design artifacts into code, eliminating manual drift.
- **Shared Registry & CI** publish and consume design tokens as code packages.
- A **dedicated feedback channel** closes the loop, enabling rapid iteration and alignment.

8.4 Roadmap Planning and Backlog Prioritization

Goal Statement
In this section you'll learn how to align your design-system's development with product goals—by creating a clear roadmap, prioritizing backlog items (new features, bug fixes, documentation), and communicating timelines to stakeholders—ensuring that the library evolves in a focused, value-driven way.

Key Terms

- **Roadmap**
- **Backlog**
- **Prioritization Framework (RICE, MoSCoW)**
- **Stakeholder Alignment**
- **Release Milestones**

Practical Outcome
By the end, you'll have a templated roadmap document and a prioritized backlog in your issue tracker, organized by quarter or version, with clear criteria for what gets done next and when—helping teams plan sprints around the most impactful design-system work.

Research & Gather Notes

- **Official Docs & Blogs**
  - Atlassian's guide on "Product Roadmaps".
  - Intercom's "RICE Method" for prioritization.
- **Community Examples**
  - GitHub: Open-source design-system roadmaps (e.g., Chakra UI's public planning issues).
  - Blog: "How Shopify maintains their Polaris roadmap and backlog."
- **Your Own Experience**
  - Learned that combining **RICE scoring** (Reach, Impact, Confidence, Effort) with **MoSCoW** (Must, Should, Could, Won't) helps balance quick wins and strategic initiatives.
  - Found that a living **roadmap board** in Jira or GitHub Projects fosters transparency and accountability.

A design system must evolve to meet changing product needs, accessibility standards, and developer feedback. A **roadmap** lays out planned themes or milestones—such as "v2.0: Theming Overhaul" or "Accessibility Enhancements Q4"—while a **backlog** houses all candidate tasks. Effective **prioritization frameworks** like **RICE** (estimating Reach, Impact, Confidence, Effort) or **MoSCoW** classification (Must, Should, Could, Won't) turn a chaotic list into a focused action plan. Communicating your roadmap to designers, developers, and business stakeholders builds trust and aligns expectations.

Concept Breakdown

1. **Roadmap**
   - High-level view of upcoming releases or thematic areas, typically organized by quarter or version.
2. **Backlog**
   - A triaged list of issues, features, and improvements, each with metadata (priority, estimate, owner).
3. **RICE Scoring**
   - Quantitative prioritization:
     - **Reach:** number of users affected
     - **Impact:** how much value per user
     - **Confidence:** confidence in your estimates
     - **Effort:** team weeks or story points
     - Score = (Reach × Impact × Confidence) / Effort

4. **MoSCoW Method**
    - Qualitative classification:
        - **Must Have**: critical for next release
        - **Should Have**: important but not critical
        - **Could Have**: nice to have if time allows
        - **Won't Have**: deferred for now
5. **Stakeholder Alignment**
    - Regular roadmap reviews with product managers, designers, and engineering leads to adjust priorities based on business goals.

---

4. Roadmap & Backlog Example

```
# Design System Roadmap 2025

## Q3 2025 (v2.0)
- Theming Overhaul (Must)
- Accessibility Enhancements (Must)
- Documentation Portal Migration (Should)

## Q4 2025 (v2.1)
- Composite Pattern Library (Should)
- Fluid Typography Tweaks (Could)
- Playwright Integration for E2E (Won't)


# Backlog (RICE-Scored)
```

Issue	Reach	Impact	Confidence	Effort	RICE Score	Priority
Dark Mode Token Overrides	5000	3	0.8	2	6000	High (1)
Storybook Performance Audit	2000	2	0.7	3	933	Medium (3)
CI Pipeline Caching	1000	1	0.9	1	900	High (2)
Theme Editor Export JSON	1500	1	0.6	2	450	Low (4)

Common Pitfalls

1. **Overloading Roadmap**
   - Trying to plan too many features dilutes focus.
   - **Fix:** Limit each quarter to a few Must-Have initiatives.
2. **Neglecting Estimates**
   - Without effort estimates, prioritization is wishful thinking.
   - **Fix:** Involve developers in rough sizing (story points or team-weeks).
3. **Lack of Visibility**
   - Stakeholders feel out of the loop if the roadmap isn't public.
   - **Fix:** Publish the roadmap in a shared board (e.g., GitHub Projects, Jira) and review it quarterly.

Hands-On Exercise

Objective: Create your initial roadmap and prioritize your backlog.

1. **Draft Roadmap:**
   - Identify three major themes or releases for the next two quarters.
   - Classify each as Must, Should, Could, or Won't.
2. **Compile Backlog:**
   - List 8–10 candidate tasks (features, fixes, docs).
   - Estimate Reach, Impact (1–5), Confidence (0.5–1), and Effort (1–5) for each.
3. **Compute RICE Scores:**
   - Calculate scores and sort the backlog by descending score.
4. **Publish & Review:**
   - Create a shared board (e.g., GitHub Project) with your roadmap and backlog columns.
   - Invite a designer and PM to review and adjust priorities.
5. **Deliverable:**
   - A markdown or board view of your roadmap and a prioritized backlog table.
   - Screenshots or a link to the board showing RICE scores and classifications.

7. End-of-Section Summary

- A **roadmap** outlines high-level release themes by quarter or version.
- A **prioritized backlog**—using RICE or MoSCoW—focuses your team on the most impactful work.
- Regular **stakeholder reviews** ensure alignment and adaptability as business needs evolve.

Visual Aid: Governance Process Flowchart

```
Governance Process Flowchart

┌───────────────────┐
│  Propose Change   │
│ (Issue or PR)     │
└─────────┬─────────┘
          │
          ▼
┌───────────────────┐
│  Triage & Label   │
│ (Priority, Area)  │
└─────────┬─────────┘
          │
          ▼
┌──────────────────────────┐
│  Developer Review        │
│ - Code quality           │
│ - Automated checks pass  │
└─────────┬────────────────┘
          │
          ▼
┌──────────────────────────┐
│  Design & UX Review      │
│ - Visual QA (Chromatic)  │
│ - Accessibility (axe)    │
└─────────┬────────────────┘
          │
          ▼
┌──────────────────────────┐
│  Governance Board Review │
│ - Align with roadmap     │
│ - Regulatory compliance  │
└─────────┬────────────────┘
          │
          ▼
```

```
┌─────────────────────┐
│     Approval &      │
│   Merge to Main     │
└─────────────────────┘
          │
          │
          ▼
┌─────────────────────┐
│  Release Pipeline   │
│ (CI/CD → npm, Docs) │
└─────────────────────┘
```

8.5 End-of-Chapter Summary & Key Takeaways

1. **Contribution Guidelines**
   - A well-crafted **CONTRIBUTING.md**, along with issue/PR templates and commit-lint hooks, sets clear expectations for reporting bugs, proposing features, writing code, and following Conventional Commits—smoothing onboarding and ensuring consistency.
2. **Code Review & Visual QA**
   - Automate technical checks (lint, tests, a11y scans, visual regression) in CI, supplement with a concise PR checklist, and require both developer and designer approvals—catching functional and visual regressions before merge.
3. **Design–Dev Hand-Offs**
   - Maintain a **versioned Figma library**, export design tokens via plugins, publish them as code packages, and consume them in builds—closing the loop with a dedicated feedback channel to prevent design-code drift.
4. **Roadmap & Backlog Prioritization**
   - Use high-level **roadmaps** (by quarter or version) to communicate key themes, and quantitative frameworks like **RICE** or qualitative MoSCoW to score and sequence backlog items—aligning design-system evolution with business impact and stakeholder expectations.
5. **Governance Workflow**
   - Define a clear governance process: issue triage, developer review, design/UX validation, governance-board alignment, and automated CI/CD releases—ensuring every change is vetted for quality, consistency, and strategic fit.

With these collaboration, governance, and scaling practices in place, your design system is primed for sustainable growth, broad adoption, and continuous improvement across teams and projects.

8.6 Hands-On Exercises

Exercise 1: Publish and Enforce Your Contribution Guidelines

- **Objective:** Make your CONTRIBUTING.md, issue templates, and PR templates live, and enforce them in your repo.
- **Steps:**
    1. Add `CONTRIBUTING.md` to your repo root (with sections from 8.1).
    2. Create `.github/ISSUE_TEMPLATE/bug_report.md` and `feature_request.md`.
    3. Create `.github/PULL_REQUEST_TEMPLATE.md` including the PR checklist.
    4. Install and configure `@commitlint/config-conventional` with a Husky pre-commit hook.
    5. Open a test issue and a test PR to verify the templates appear, and commit with an invalid message to ensure commit-lint blocks it.
- **Deliverable:**
    - A GitHub repo where the issue and PR templates render automatically, and an attempt to commit a non-conventional message is prevented.

Exercise 2: Configure and Validate Your Code Review & Visual QA Workflow

- **Objective:** Integrate automated checks—lint, tests, a11y, and Chromatic—into your PR process and require human sign-off.
- **Steps:**
    1. Update your GitHub Actions CI (`ci.yml`) to include jobs for `npm run lint`, `npm test --ci`, and `npx axe`.
    2. Ensure your visual-regression workflow (Chromatic) is running on each PR.

3. Add branch protection rules requiring passing statuses for `lint`, `test`, and `visual-diff`, plus at least one reviewer approval.
4. Create a sample PR that intentionally breaks an a11y rule or visual style; confirm the CI fails and you cannot merge until fixes and approvals are in place.

- **Deliverable:**
  - A PR showing failing checks for an introduced error, then updated code passing all checks and obtaining required approvals.

Exercise 3: Automate Token Exports and Consumption for Design–Dev Handoff

- **Objective:** Set up an end-to-end pipeline exporting tokens from your design-tokens repo and consuming them in your design-system codebase.
- **Steps:**
  1. In a separate `design-tokens` repo, commit a sample JSON of your color and spacing tokens.
  2. Add a GitHub Action that, on push to `main`, publishes the JSON as an npm package (`@your-org/design-tokens@<version>`).
  3. In your design-system repo, add `@your-org/design-tokens` as a dependency and configure a build script (e.g. with Style Dictionary) to generate CSS variables and TS types from the JSON.
  4. Trigger a token change: bump version, export new JSON, publish, update your design-system dependency, rebuild, and verify new values appear in your components.
- **Deliverable:**
  - Screenshots or logs showing the token-repo Action publishing a new version, and your design-system build picking up and rendering the updated tokens.

Exercise 4: Create Your Roadmap and Prioritize Backlog with RICE or MoSCoW

- **Objective:** Develop a clear roadmap document and a scored backlog to guide your design-system's upcoming work.
- **Steps:**
    1. Identify 3 major themes or releases for the next two quarters; classify each with MoSCoW (Must, Should, Could, Won't).
    2. List 8–10 candidate tasks (features, improvements, bugs) in your issue tracker.
    3. For each task, estimate Reach, Impact (1–5), Confidence (0.5–1), and Effort (1–5), then compute the RICE score.
    4. Create or update a GitHub Project board with columns for **Roadmap** and **Backlog**, populating cards with your priorities and annotations.
    5. Invite a product manager or designer to review and adjust as needed.
- **Deliverable:**
    - A public roadmap document (Markdown or board link) and a backlog table sorted by RICE score, with labels indicating MoSCoW classification.

Exercise 5: Define and Simulate Your Governance Workflow

- **Objective:** Implement the governance process flowchart in your repo and simulate a change going through each stage.
- **Steps:**
    1. Add your flowchart diagram and a narrative of the governance steps to your `GOVERNANCE.md`.
    2. Create GitHub labels (`needs-triage`, `needs-dev-review`, `needs-design-review`, `needs-gov-review`).
    3. Open a mock issue or PR and manually apply each label in sequence, documenting in the issue's comments when each review step is completed.
    4. Configure branch protection to require that PRs have the `needs-dev-review` and `needs-design-review` checks pass before merge.
    5. Upon merge, ensure your CI release pipeline triggers automatically.

- **Deliverable:**
  - A `GOVERNANCE.md` in your repo, demo issue/PR showing labels applied in order, and evidence of CI release running on merge.

These exercises will cement your collaboration, governance, and scaling practices—ensuring your design system thrives in a structured, cross-functional environment.

8.7 Next Steps: Drafting Your First Design-Dev RFC

Goal Statement
In this section you'll learn how to author a **Request for Comments (RFC)** document to propose significant design-system changes—such as a new theming API or governance update—gather cross-functional feedback, and drive consensus before implementation.

Key Terms

- **RFC**
- **Proposal Template**
- **Stakeholder Review**
- **Migration Plan**
- **Consensus**

Practical Outcome
By the end, you'll have a templated RFC in your repo (e.g. `rfcs/0001-new-theming-architecture.md`), know how to structure its sections, circulate it for feedback, and shepherd it to approval—establishing a transparent decision-making process for major changes.

Explanatory Text

Major changes—like overhauling your theming strategy, deprecating components, or altering your versioning workflow—impact many teams and codebases. An **RFC**:

- Captures **motivation** and **background** for the change
- Defines the **proposed solution** with API sketches and examples
- Lists **alternatives considered** and trade-offs
- Outlines **impact** and a **migration plan**
- Invites **reviewers** (designers, developers, product) to comment
- Creates an **audit trail** of decisions

Using an RFC ensures that large-scale decisions are debated openly, documented thoroughly, and implemented with consensus.

RFC Template Structure

```
# RFC 0001: [Short Descriptive Title]
**Status:** Draft
**Author:** Your Name
**Date:** YYYY-MM-DD

## 1. Background & Motivation
Why is this change needed? What pain points or user stories
drive it?

## 2. Proposal
High-level overview, API sketches, code examples, or
diagrams.

## 3. Alternatives Considered
List other approaches, with pros/cons and reasons for
rejection.

## 4. Impact & Migration Plan
Which components and projects are affected? Step-by-step
migration or dual-support strategy.

## 5. Drawbacks & Unresolved Questions
Known limitations or areas needing further exploration.

## 6. Appendices & References
Links to prototypes, design files, related issues or RFCs.

## 7. Reviewers
- @design-lead
```

```
- @frontend-team
- @product-manager
```

Hands-On Exercise

Objective: Draft your first RFC for a non-trivial change.

1. **Select a Topic**
   Choose an upcoming change, e.g. "Adopt Component-Level Container Queries" or "Switch to CSS-in-JS."
2. **Create the RFC File**
   In your repo's `rfcs/` folder, add `0002-your-topic.md` using the template above.
3. **Populate All Sections**
   Write background, proposal details, alternatives, impact plan, and list reviewers.
4. **Circulate for Feedback**
   Open a PR against `main`, tag stakeholders, and request comments.
5. **Revise & Finalize**
   Incorporate feedback, update **Status** to "Accepted," and merge the RFC.

Summary

- An **RFC** formalizes major design-system proposals, ensuring transparent, documented decision-making.
- A clear **template** guides authors to cover background, proposal, alternatives, impact, and migration.
- Circulating the RFC as a PR invites cross-functional review and builds consensus before implementation.

Chapter 9: Case Studies and Real-World Examples

9.1 How Acme Corp Reduced UI Bugs by 70%

Goal Statement
In this case study you'll learn how Acme Corp leveraged a React design system—complete with Storybook-driven development, visual regression testing, and strict governance—to slash UI bugs by 70%, speeding delivery and improving user satisfaction.

Key Terms

- **Visual Regression Testing**
- **Component-Driven Development**
- **Design System Adoption**
- **Governance Workflow**
- **Bug Metrics**

Practical Outcome
By the end, you'll understand the strategies Acme Corp used—incremental migration, automated QA, and clear governance—to measure, track, and reduce UI defects, and you'll be able to apply similar tactics in your organization.

Research & Gather Notes

- **Official Sources**
  - Internal postmortem reports from Acme Corp's UX team.
  - GitHub commit history showing introduction of Storybook and Chromatic.
- **Community Examples**
  - Conference talk "Scaling React at Acme Corp" (React Summit 2024).
  - Blog articles on "Design Systems in the Enterprise" highlighting Acme's workflow.
- **Your Own Experience**

- Noted that visibility into component regressions via visual tests often catches layout shifts that unit tests miss.
- Saw similar improvements at clients who enforced strict PR templates and design reviews.

Acme Corp maintained a large React application with dozens of screens and hundreds of UI components. Fragmented styling, ad-hoc fixes, and inconsistent testing led to an annual backlog of over 200 UI bugs—ranging from misaligned buttons to theme regressions. By introducing a unified design system and rigorous QA pipeline, Acme reduced their UI bug rate by 70% within six months.

Key pillars of their approach included:

1. **Component-Driven Development (CDD):** All new UI built as isolated components in Storybook.
2. **Visual Regression Testing:** Chromatic scans caught subtle style changes before merge.
3. **Governance & Metrics:** Defined UI-bug tracking metrics and integrated them into sprint retrospectives.
4. **Incremental Migration:** Legacy screens were strangled gradually, replacing brittle CSS with tokens and approved components.

Concept Breakdown

1. **Component-Driven Development**
    - Encourages building and testing components in isolation, improving reusability and catch bugs early.
2. **Visual Regression Testing**
    - Automated snapshot comparisons surfaced unintended visual changes—alignments, colors, spacing.
3. **Governance Workflow**
    - Enforced PR templates, required design and dev approvals, and tracked “UI Bug” labels in their issue tracker.
4. **Bug Metrics**
    - Acme measured number of UI bugs reported per sprint and trending visual diff failures, setting a KPI to reduce bugs by 20% quarter-over-quarter.
5. **Incremental Migration**
    - Used path aliases and ESLint warnings to guide developers off legacy code, migrating one screen per sprint.

Code Walkthrough

While Acme's full codebase is proprietary, their high-level implementation looked like this:

```
# Example: adding Chromatic visual regression to CI
npx chromatic --project-token $CHROMATIC_TOKEN --exit-zero-
on-changes
# GitHub Actions snippet
jobs:
  chromatic:
    runs-on: ubuntu-latest
    steps:
      - uses: actions/checkout@v3
      - run: npm ci
      - run: npm run build-storybook
      - env:
          CHROMATIC_TOKEN: ${{ secrets.CHROMATIC_TOKEN }}
        run: npm run chromatic
```

They paired this with:

```
// ESLint rule to warn on legacy imports
"no-restricted-imports": [
  "warn",
  { "patterns": ["src/legacy/*"] }
]
```

And a Storybook decorator:

```
// .storybook/preview.js
import { ThemeProvider } from '@acme/design-system';
export const decorators = [(Story) =>
<ThemeProvider><Story/></ThemeProvider>];
```

```
Acme Corp UI Bug Reduction Timeline

Sprint →
┌────────┐    ┌────────┐    ┌────────┐
│ Q1     │    │ Q2     │    │ Q3     │
│ 200 UI │    │ 120 UI │    │  60 UI │
│ bugs   │    │ bugs   │    │ bugs   │
└────────┘    └────────┘    └────────┘
     ↓             ↓             ↓
 CDD & Visual  Governance   Legacy
 Testing setup   & Metrics    Migration
```

Hands-On Exercise

Objective: Emulate Acme's approach to reduce UI bugs in your project.

1. **Baseline Measurement:**
   - Tally UI-related bug issues (labels: `ui-bug`) filed in the last quarter.
2. **Introduce Storybook & Chromatic:**
   - Scaffold Storybook, add Chromatic with `--exit-zero-on-changes`.
3. **Enforce Governance:**
   - Add PR templates requiring designers to review visual diffs.
   - Track UI-bug count each sprint and set a reduction goal.
4. **Migrate One Screen:**
   - Use path aliases to swap legacy components with design-system atoms.
   - Verify no visual regressions via Chromatic.
5. **Measure Impact:**
   - After one month, compare the number of new UI bugs reported.

Deliverable:

- A chart or table of bug counts before and after six weeks.
- Screenshots of Chromatic diffs catching a visual issue.

Summary

- **Isolation & Testing:** Building UI in Storybook and running visual-regression tests catches issues early.
- **Governance:** PR templates and required reviews standardize quality gates.
- **Data-Driven Goals:** Tracking UI-bug metrics provides clear KPIs and drives continuous improvement.
- **Incremental Migration:** Phased replacement of legacy code minimizes risk while modernizing UI.

By adopting these strategies, Acme Corp achieved a dramatic 70% reduction in UI defects—demonstrating the power of a mature, well-governed React design system.

9.2 Scaling from 10 to 100 Components in Two Months

Goal Statement
In this case study you'll see how BetaWorks accelerated their React design system from an initial 10 core components to a robust library of 100+ components in just eight weeks—achieving broad feature coverage and high adoption across teams.

Key Terms

- **Component Inventory**
- **Design Tokens**
- **Automated Scaffolding**
- **Storybook-First Workflow**
- **Team Rotation**

Practical Outcome
By the end, you'll understand the practices BetaWorks employed—centralized planning, automation, parallelization, and a Storybook-driven development workflow—to scale component output without sacrificing quality or consistency.

Research & Gather Notes

- **Official Sources**
  - Internal retrospective documents from BetaWorks.
  - Conference talk "Rapid Component Growth at BetaWorks" (React Conf 2024).
- **Community Examples**
  - Blog: "How We Built Our Design System in a Month" from Acme Design.
  - GitHub: Cobra UI's generator scripts for component scaffolding.
- **Your Own Experience**

- Found that generating boilerplate via templates and codemods lets teams focus on implementation details rather than setup.
- Noted that rotating engineers through a component "bootcamp" fosters shared ownership and accelerates output.

BetaWorks launched their design system with ten foundational components—buttons, inputs, cards, modals, etc.—but product roadmaps demanded a hundred tailored UI pieces rapidly. To meet this goal, they adopted a multi-pronged strategy:

1. **Comprehensive Component Roadmap:** Cataloging 100+ needed components and grouping them by complexity and priority.
2. **Automated Scaffolding:** Using a code generator to spin up new component directories, Storybook stories, and test stubs.
3. **Parallel Team Rotation:** Small cross-functional pods each owned a subset of components, rotating every two weeks to spread knowledge.
4. **Storybook-First Development:** Every component began life as a Storybook story, ensuring documentation, edge-case stories, and visual tests from day one.
5. **Centralized Token Usage:** Strict enforcement of design tokens guaranteed consistent styling across rapidly produced components.

This approach allowed BetaWorks to scale output tenfold in two months without quality regressions or style drift.

Concept Breakdown

1. **Component Inventory & Prioritization**
   - Maintained a spreadsheet of all desired components, scored by usage frequency and complexity.
2. **Automated Scaffolding**
   - CLI tool (`create-component`) that prompts for name, generates `Component.tsx`, `Component.stories.tsx`, `Component.module.css`, test file, and entry in the index barrel.
3. **Parallelization via Teams**
   - Three rotating pods of 2–3 engineers each; each pod tackled a component group (atoms, molecules, organisms).

4. **Storybook-First Workflow**
    - Developers wrote the "happy path" story and edge-case stories before implementation, then built to satisfy them.
5. **Token-Driven Consistency**
    - Lint rules forbade hard-coded colors or spacing; all style values had to reference `tokens`.

Code Walkthrough

```
# Example scaffold command
npx create-component ButtonGroup
```

Generates:

```
src/components/atoms/ButtonGroup/
  ├── ButtonGroup.tsx
  ├── ButtonGroup.stories.tsx
  ├── ButtonGroup.module.css
  ├── ButtonGroup.test.tsx
  └── index.ts
// ButtonGroup.stories.tsx
import React from 'react';
import { ButtonGroup } from './ButtonGroup';
export default { title: 'Atoms/ButtonGroup', component:
ButtonGroup };

export const Default = () => (
  <ButtonGroup options={['Yes','No','Maybe']}
onSelect={console.log}/>
);

export const Disabled = () => (
  <ButtonGroup options={['A','B']} onSelect={console.log}
disabled />
);
// ButtonGroup.tsx (simplified)
import React from 'react';
import styles from './ButtonGroup.module.css';
import { tokens } from '../../styles/tokens';

export interface ButtonGroupProps {
  options: string[];
  onSelect: (opt: string) => void;
  disabled?: boolean;
}
```

```
export function ButtonGroup({ options, onSelect,
disabled=false }: ButtonGroupProps) {
  return (
    <div className={styles.group}>
      {options.map(opt => (
        <button
          key={opt}
          className={styles.button}
          style={{ marginRight: tokens.spacing[1] }}
          disabled={disabled}
          onClick={() => onSelect(opt)}
        >
          {opt}
        </button>
      ))}
    </div>
  );
}
```

BetaWorks' generator also wired up:

- **Index Barrel:** Automatic export in `src/components/index.ts`.
- **Test Stub:** Basic render test in `ButtonGroup.test.tsx`.

```
Scaling Workflow

┌────────────┐    ┌─────────────┐    ┌──────────────┐
│ Component  │    │ CLI Scaffold│    │ Storybook    │
│ Inventory  │➔──▸│ generate files│➔──▸│ stories/tests│
└────────────┘    └─────────────┘    └──────────────┘
                                            │
                     ┌────────────────────────────────────────────┐
                     │ Parallel Pods implement & review components│
                     └────────────────────────────────────────────┘
```

Hands-On Exercise

Objective: Emulate BetaWorks' rapid scaling approach in your project.

1. **Create Component Inventory:**
   - List 20 components your system lacks, categorized by complexity.
2. **Build a Scaffolding Script:**
   - Write a simple Node.js or Shell script that, given a component name, creates a directory with template files for `.tsx`, `.stories.tsx`, `.module.css`, and `.test.tsx`.
3. **Run a Sprint:**

   - Form two small teams; each runs your scaffold for five components, implements them via Storybook-first, and merges PRs within one week.
4. **Enforce Tokens:**
   - Add an ESLint rule or regex check that forbids hard-coded style values in new components.
5. **Deliverable:**
   - The scaffolding script in your repo.
   - A PR with five newly scaffolded and implemented components, each with Storybook stories and tests.

End-of-Section Summary

- **Centralized Planning:** A clear inventory and priority list drives focused work.
- **Automation:** Scaffolding scripts eliminate repetitive setup, freeing devs for core logic.
- **Parallel Teams:** Small pods working in parallel accelerate throughput while sharing knowledge.
- **Storybook-First:** Writing stories before code ensures documentation and edge cases are baked in.
- **Token Enforcement:** Lint rules guarantee stylistic consistency at scale.

By adopting these practices, BetaWorks successfully expanded their component library by 10× in just two months—maintaining high quality and consistency throughout.

9.3 Open-Source Design System: Lessons from the Community

Goal Statement
In this case study you'll discover key insights from leading open-source React design systems—such as Chakra UI, Material-UI, and Ant Design—and learn community best practices around governance, accessibility, theming, and ecosystem building that you can apply to your own library.

Key Terms

- **Community Governance**
- **Theming API**
- **Accessibility Compliance**
- **Plugin Ecosystem**
- **Contributor Onboarding**

Practical Outcome
By the end, you'll be able to benchmark your design system against community standards, adopt proven governance models, and implement extensibility patterns—ensuring your library thrives both within and beyond your organization.

Research & Gather Notes

- **Chakra UI**
  - **Theming API:** Uses style props and `extendTheme` for deep overrides.
  - **Accessibility:** Built-in focus management and ARIA defaults.
  - **Governance:** Clear CONTRIBUTING.md, Discord community, regular RFCs.
- **Material-UI (MUI)**
  - **Component Variants:** Support for `variant` and `color` props on most components.
  - **Plugin Ecosystem:** Official labs, pickers, data-grid packages.
  - **Versioning:** Major v4→v5 migration guided by codemods and detailed upgrade docs.
- **Ant Design**
  - **Design Tokens:** Exposed via Less variables and JSON token files.
  - **Internationalization:** Built-in i18n support for multiple locales.
  - **Community:** Large contributor base, monthly roadmaps, and transparency via GitHub Projects.

Open-source design systems succeed through robust community engagement, flexible theming, and relentless focus on accessibility. Projects like Chakra UI, MUI, and Ant Design offer lessons in how to structure governance, design extensible APIs, and build vibrant ecosystems of plugins and extensions.

Key takeaways include:

1. **Governance Through RFCs & Roadmaps**
   - Chakra UI uses GitHub Discussions for RFCs; MUI publishes quarterly roadmaps; Ant Design solicits community feedback on GitHub Projects.
2. **Extensible Theming APIs**
   - `extendTheme` patterns (Chakra) and theme augmentation (MUI) allow users to override deeply nested tokens without copying entire theme objects.
3. **Accessibility by Default**
   - ARIA roles, focus styles, keyboard handlers built into each component—ensuring compliance without extra effort.
4. **Ecosystem of Plugins & Add-Ons**
   - Official "labs" packages (MUI X), community-contributed components, and first-class plugin APIs keep core libraries lean while serving diverse needs.
5. **Onboarding & Documentation**
   - Comprehensive docs websites with live playgrounds, migration guides (v4→v5 for MUI), and easy setup instructions lower the barrier to entry.

```
Community Best Practices Matrix
```

Practice	Chakra UI	MUI	Ant Design
Theming	extendTheme	createTheme	Less tokens
Accessibility	useA11y hooks	built-in ARIA	focus & roles
Governance	RFCs/Discus.	Roadmaps	GitHub Projects
Extensibility	style props	slot props	plugin APIs
Migration Support	N/A	codemods	upgrade guide

Hands-On Exercise

Objective: Incorporate a community-inspired best practice into your design system.

1. **Select a Practice:**
   - Choose one area (governance, theming, accessibility, or extensibility).
2. **Implement a Feature:**
   - **Governance:** Add a "Propose an RFC" GitHub Discussion template and process.
   - **Theming:** Build an `extendTheme` helper that deeply merges default tokens with user overrides.
   - **Accessibility:** Integrate `@chakra-ui/a11y` hooks or similar ARIA utilities into your components.
   - **Extensibility:** Define a plugin API (e.g., `usePlugin`) to let consumers register custom component variants.
3. **Document & Share:**
   - Update your documentation site with a new section explaining the feature and usage examples.
   - Solicit feedback via your project's community channel (Slack/Discord/GitHub Discussions).
4. **Deliverable:**
   - A PR implementing the chosen feature, plus updated docs and a link to community feedback.

Summary

- Open-source libraries excel by combining strong governance, flexible theming, and built-in accessibility.
- Building an ecosystem of plugins and providing smooth migration paths fosters adoption and longevity.
- By borrowing and adapting these community best practices, your design system can achieve similar scale, quality, and contributor engagement.

Before-and-After Component Diff

Component	Before	After
Button	html <button style="padding:8px; background:#0055FF; color:#FFF;">Click</button>	jsx <Button variant="primary" size="medium">Click</Button>Uses design-system <Button> with token-driven padding, colors, and built-in props.
Card	html <div className="legacy-card"><h3>Title</h3><p>Content</p></div>	jsx <Card elevation="sm" padding="md">…</Card>Uses <Card> composite with spacing and elevation tokens and semantic API.
TextInput	html <input type="text" style="border:1px solid #CCC; padding:4px;" />	jsx <TextInput label="Name" placeholder="Your name" />Uses <TextInput> atom with tokenized border, spacing, label, and built-in accessibility.

End-of-Chapter Summary & Key Takeaways

1. **Measurable Impact Through QA**
    - Adopting Component-Driven Development and visual regression testing (e.g., Chromatic) can dramatically reduce UI defects, as Acme Corp's 70% bug reduction demonstrates.
2. **Rapid Component Scaling**
    - Centralized planning, automated scaffolding, parallel team efforts, and a Storybook-first workflow enabled BetaWorks to grow from 10 to 100+ components in two months without sacrificing consistency.
3. **Community Best Practices**
    - Leading open-source design systems (Chakra UI, MUI, Ant Design) showcase governance via RFCs and roadmaps, extensible theming APIs, accessibility by default, and vibrant plugin ecosystems—models you can adapt to your project.
4. **Consistency via Tokens and Templates**

    - Enforcing strict use of design tokens and component templates ensures stylistic and behavioral uniformity, whether you're migrating legacy code or onboarding new contributors.
5. **Continuous Learning & Iteration**
    - Case studies highlight the value of data-driven goals (bug metrics, RICE scores), incremental migrations, and community feedback loops—practices that keep a design system healthy and evolving.

9.5 Hands-On Exercises

Exercise 1: Measure and Reduce Your UI Bug Rate

- **Objective:** Establish a baseline of UI bugs and implement visual regression tests to drive down defect count.
- **Steps:**
    1. Tally all open "UI Bug"–labeled issues in your tracker over the past quarter.
    2. Integrate Chromatic (or an equivalent visual-regression tool) into your CI pipeline with `--exit-zero-on-changes`.
    3. Cause a deliberate visual change (e.g. tweak a button's padding) and confirm the snapshot test fails.
    4. Fix the change to restore baseline visuals and merge.
    5. After two weeks of running tests on every PR, re-count new UI bugs filed.
- **Deliverable:**
    - A before/after table of UI-bug counts.
    - A screenshot of a failed visual-diff and its resolution.

Exercise 2: Rapidly Scaffold and Implement 10 Components

- **Objective:** Practice BetaWorks' scaling approach by generating and building ten new components in one week.
- **Steps:**
    1. Create a simple scaffolding script (`create-component`) that generates the folder and template files (`.tsx`, `.stories.tsx`, `.module.css`, `.test.tsx`).

2. Use your script to scaffold ten component names from your backlog.
3. For each, write at least one "happy-path" and one "edge-case" Storybook story before implementation.
4. Implement each component to satisfy its stories, using your design tokens exclusively for styling.

- **Deliverable:**
  - The scaffolding script in your repo.
  - A PR containing ten fully implemented components with stories and tests.

Exercise 3: Adopt a Community Best Practice

- **Objective:** Pick a proven pattern from Chakra UI, MUI, or Ant Design and integrate it into your library.
- **Options (choose one):**
  - **Theming API:** Implement an `extendTheme` helper to deep-merge default tokens with overrides.
  - **Accessibility Defaults:** Add built-in ARIA roles and keyboard support to a core component.
  - **Plugin Architecture:** Expose a plugin registration API that allows consumers to add custom variants.
- **Steps:**

  0. Research the chosen project's implementation.
  1. Implement the feature in your library and update documentation with usage examples.
  2. Write a Storybook story or MDX doc showcasing the new capability.

- **Deliverable:**
  - A PR implementing the feature, updated docs, and a working Storybook demo.

Exercise 4: Create a Before-and-After Diff Report

- **Objective:** Demonstrate the impact of migrating a legacy component to your design system.
- **Steps:**
    1. Identify a small legacy component (e.g., a card or input) in your app and capture its existing markup and styling.
    2. Replace it with your design-system equivalent (e.g., `<Card>` or `<TextInput>`), removing all inline styles.
    3. Use Chromatic or a screenshot tool to capture "before" and "after" images.
    4. Present a markdown table summarizing the diff (`Before` vs. `After`) and noting benefits (accessibility, consistency, reduced CSS).
- **Deliverable:**
    - A markdown file or PR description containing the diff table and before/after screenshots.

These exercises will help you apply the lessons from real-world case studies—measuring impact, scaling output, leveraging community patterns, and showcasing the value of your design system in concrete before/after comparisons.

9.6 Next Steps: Adapting Lessons to Your Team

Goal Statement
In this section you'll learn how to tailor the strategies and patterns covered in this chapter—bug reduction, rapid scaling, and community best practices—to the unique context, size, and goals of your team.

Key Terms

- **Team Assessment**
- **Pilot Projects**
- **Feedback Loops**
- **Custom Tooling**
- **Continuous Improvement**

Practical Outcome
By the end, you'll have an actionable plan for introducing these case-study practices in pilots, gathering metrics, refining processes, and scaling what works across your organization.

---

2. Explanatory Text

Every team has its own constraints—headcount, product cadence, legacy debt, and cultural norms. To successfully adapt the learnings:

1. **Assess Your Starting Point**
   - Audit your current component library: number of components, test coverage, CI checks, and open UI-bug backlog.
   - Survey team familiarity with Storybook, visual-regression tools, and design-system concepts.
2. **Define Pilot Goals**
   - Pick one practice to introduce first (e.g., visual regression testing or scaffolding automation).
   - Set clear success metrics (e.g., "catch 90% of visual regressions before merge," or "scaffold and ship 5 new components this sprint").
3. **Run an Iterative Pilot**
   - Form a small cross-functional task force.
   - Time-box the pilot (e.g., two sprints) and document pain points, wins, and blockers.
4. **Gather and Share Metrics**
   - Track CI pass rates, bug counts, component throughput, and team sentiment.
   - Present before/after data in a short demo or "lunch-and-learn" to build buy-in.
5. **Refine Processes and Tooling**
   - Based on pilot feedback, tweak your CI config, PR templates, or scaffolding scripts.
   - Automate repetitive steps (e.g., lint-rules, token exports) where gaps emerge.
6. **Scale Incrementally**
   - Expand successful pilots to more teams or projects.
   - Formalize new practices in your CONTRIBUTING.md, governance docs, and onboarding materials.

7. **Establish Continuous Feedback**
    - Regularly review metrics (monthly or quarterly).
    - Create a feedback channel (Slack, standup agenda) for ongoing suggestions and issues.

---

3. Hands-On Exercise

Objective: Kick off a pilot to adapt one case-study practice in your team.

1. **Select a Practice:**
    - Choose either visual-regression testing (e.g., Chromatic), automated scaffolding, or token-driven styling.
2. **Define Success Metrics:**
    - E.g., "Reduce visual regressions merged by 50% in next sprint" or "Scaffold 3 new components in one week."
3. **Execute Pilot:**
    - Configure your CI or tooling for that practice.
    - Use it on new or existing components for two sprints.
4. **Collect Data:**
    - Record bug counts, story throughput, or CI failure rates before and after.
5. **Report Findings:**
    - Prepare a one-page summary with metrics, lessons learned, and recommendations for broader rollout.

---

4. End-of-Section Summary

- **Start Small:** Pilot one high-impact practice to minimize risk and surface challenges early.
- **Measure Everything:** Define clear metrics to quantify success and guide decision-making.
- **Iterate Quickly:** Use feedback loops to refine tooling and processes before scaling.
- **Document & Share:** Codify what works—updating docs, templates, and training—to embed practices across your team.

With a structured pilot and data-driven refinement, you'll transform these real-world lessons into enduring improvements for your own design system.

Chapter 10: Future Trends in React Design Systems

10.1 Server Components and Edge Rendering

Goal Statement
In this section you'll learn how React's emerging **Server Components** and **Edge Rendering** patterns can optimize performance, reduce bundle sizes, and enable dynamic UI at the network edge—paving the way for ultra-fast, scalable React design systems.

Key Terms

- **React Server Components (RSC)**
- **Edge Rendering**
- **Streaming SSR**
- **Islands Architecture**
- **Cold Starts**

Practical Outcome
By the end, you'll understand when and how to author components that run on the server (or edge), stream rendered HTML to clients, and selectively hydrate interactive "islands" on the browser—resulting in smaller client bundles, faster first-contentful paint, and more resilient UI.

Research & Gather Notes

- **Official Sources**
    - React RFC: "Server Components" (React 18+).
    - Vercel Edge Functions documentation and Next.js' App Router for RSC.
- **Community Examples**
    - Next.js "app" directory using Server and Client components.
    - Astro's Islands architecture illustrating partial hydration.
- **Your Own Experience**
    - Noted that offloading data fetching and layout to the server eliminates waterfall fetches and shrinks client JS.

- Saw edge functions deliver personalized UI at sub-50 ms latency globally.

Traditional React apps ship a large JavaScript bundle to the browser, then fetch data and hydrate the entire UI—delaying interactive readiness. **React Server Components (RSC)** invert that model: components annotated as `server` run on Node (or edge), fetch data directly, and emit HTML plus a minimal client payload. Coupled with **Edge Rendering**, you can execute these RSCs at CDN edge nodes—bringing UI generation geographically closer to users.

This architecture yields a **streaming SSR** experience: the server/edge streams static markup for layout and content immediately, then hydrates only interactive "islands" (client components) as needed. Design-system components can leverage this by splitting purely presentational pieces as server components (no client bundle), and marking interactive controls (forms, theme switchers) for client hydration only.

Concept Breakdown

1. **React Server Components**
   - `.server.js` files that run on the server, import data APIs directly, and never ship their code to the client.
2. **Client Components**
   - `.client.js` files hydrated in the browser to handle interactivity (e.g., onClick, state).
3. **Streaming SSR**
   - Server begins sending HTML immediately, reducing Time to First Byte (TTFB) and First Contentful Paint.
4. **Edge Rendering**
   - Executing RSCs in edge functions (e.g., Vercel, Cloudflare Workers) for global low-latency UI generation.
5. **Islands Architecture**
   - Only hydrate interactive portions ("islands") of the page, leaving static content as plain HTML.

Code Walkthrough

```
// app/components/ArticleList.server.tsx
import React from 'react';
import { getArticles } from '../lib/api';

export default async function ArticleList() {
```

```
  const articles = await getArticles();       // runs on
server/edge
  return (
    <ul>
      {articles.map(a => (
        <li key={a.id}>
          <a href={`/articles/${a.slug}`}>{a.title}</a>
        </li>
      ))}
    </ul>
  );
}
// app/components/ThemeToggle.client.tsx
'use client';
import { useTheme } from '../theme/ThemeProvider';

export function ThemeToggle() {
  const { theme, setTheme } = useTheme();   // client-side
hook
  return (
    <button onClick={() => setTheme(theme === 'light' ?
'dark' : 'light')}>
      Toggle to {theme === 'light' ? 'Dark' : 'Light'}
    </button>
  );
}
// app/page.tsx
import ArticleList from './components/ArticleList.server';
import { ThemeToggle } from
'./components/ThemeToggle.client';

export default function Page() {
  return (
    <div>
      <header><h1>Blog</h1><ThemeToggle/></header>
      <main><ArticleList/></main>
    </div>
  );
}
```

- **What it does:**
  - `ArticleList.server.tsx` fetches data at the server/edge and streams its HTML.
  - `ThemeToggle.client.tsx` hydrates only that button on the client.
  - Page combines both, yielding minimal client JS.
- **Why this approach:**
  - **Performance:** Server components don't ship data-fetching code nor React runtime to the browser.

- **Scalability:** Edge rendering reduces latency for global users.
- **Bundle Size:** Hydration island pattern dramatically shrinks JS payloads.

Common Pitfalls

1. **Over-Hydration**
    - Marking too many components as client runs more JS than necessary.
    - **Fix:** Audit interactivity: only controls and dynamic UI need client components.
2. **Edge Cold Starts**
    - Rarely-invoked edge functions may cold-start, causing latency spikes.
    - **Fix:** Keep server component code minimal and warm critical edge routes.
3. **Data Consistency**
    - Streaming SSR can yield layout shifts if CSS isn't fully loaded.
    - **Fix:** Use critical CSS inlined and consistent class names between server and client.

```
Streaming RSC & Islands

[ Edge / Server ]
┌─────────────────────────────────────────┐
│ <html>                                  │
│  <header>…</header>                     │
│  <ul>…ArticleList.server (HTML)…</ul>   │  — streamed to
client
│  <div id="theme-toggle">…</div>         │
└─────────────────────────────────────────┘
         ↓
[ Browser ]
┌─────────────────────────────────────────┐
│ HTML parsed & painted immediately       │
│                                         │
│ ┌───────────────┐                       │
│ │ React hydrates│ ThemeToggle.client    │
│ │ only in <div> │ making button live    │
│ └───────────────┘                       │
└─────────────────────────────────────────┘
```

Hands-On Exercise

Objective: Convert a static list component to a Server Component with an interactive island.

1. **Identify Component:**
   - Choose a data-driven list in your app (e.g., `<UserList>`).
2. **Refactor to Server Component:**
   - Rename to `UserList.server.tsx`, move data fetching inside, and remove client hooks.
3. **Extract an Island:**
   - If the list rows have an interactive "Follow" button, extract that into `FollowButton.client.tsx`.
4. **Integrate and Test:**
   - Render `UserList.server` and `<FollowButton.client>` island together in your page.
   - Measure first load bundle size and TTFB before and after.
5. **Deliverable:**
   - Code diff showing server/client split.
   - Metrics: bundle size reduction and hydration time improvements.

Key Takeaways

- **Server Components** allow data fetching and rendering on the server/edge, eliminating client-side overhead.
- **Client Components** hydrates only interactive parts, forming an "islands" architecture.
- **Edge Rendering** brings UI generation closer to users for sub-50 ms latency globally.

Next Steps
Proceed to **Section 10.2**, where we'll explore **Component-Level CSS Grid and Container Queries**—leveraging modern CSS features to build truly responsive, context-aware UI primitives.

10.2 Component-Level CSS Grid and Container Queries

Goal Statement
In this section you'll learn how to leverage **CSS Grid** at the component level in combination with **CSS Container Queries**—enabling components to

adapt their layout based on their own rendered size rather than global viewport breakpoints.

Key Terms

- **CSS Grid**
- **Container Queries**
- **`@container` Rule**
- **Intrinsic Sizing**
- **Layout Responsiveness**

Practical Outcome
By the end, you'll be able to author Grid-based components whose template and styling adjust automatically when their containing element crosses defined width thresholds—yielding truly modular, context-aware UI primitives.

Research & Gather Notes

- **Official Specs & Guides**
  - MDN: "CSS Container Queries" documentation.
  - CSS Working Group drafts on the `@container` rule.
- **Community Examples**
  - GitHub: Chrome Labs' demo of container-query-polyfill.
  - Blog: "Component Queries: Beyond Media Queries" by Una Kravets.
- **Your Own Experience**
  - Found that container queries unlock flexible cards that reflow internally without relying on global breakpoints.
  - Noted that combining Grid's repeat/auto-fit with container queries yields adaptive galleries and dashboards.

Traditional responsive design uses viewport-based media queries, which can misalign component behavior when placed in constrained contexts (e.g., sidebars, modals). **Container Queries** solve this by letting components observe their own container size. Paired with **CSS Grid**, you can define grid templates that shift column counts, gaps, or row sizes based on the component's rendered width.

We'll build a `<PhotoGallery>` component that displays images in a grid whose number of columns adapts when the gallery's container narrows below 600px or expands above 900px—using `@container` and Grid's `auto-fit` features. This pattern ensures each gallery instance behaves correctly regardless of where it's embedded.

Concept Breakdown

1. **CSS Grid**
   - Defines rows/columns and placement via `display: grid; grid-template-columns`.
2. **Container Queries**
   - Uses `@container <name> (min-width: <value>) { … }` to apply rules when a container meets conditions.
3. **Intrinsic Sizing**
   - Components size themselves to their content; container queries observe that size.
4. **`container-type` Property**
   - Enables query context: `container-type: inline-size;` on the component wrapper.
5. **Adaptive Layouts**
   - Combining Grid and container queries creates self-adjusting components.

Code Walkthrough

```
/* src/components/PhotoGallery/PhotoGallery.css */
.gallery {
  display: grid;
  gap: var(--spacing-2);
  /* Define container context */
  container-type: inline-size;
  container-name: gallery;
  /* Default: 2 columns */
  grid-template-columns: repeat(2, 1fr);
}

/* When container >= 600px: 3 columns */
@container gallery (min-width: 600px) {
  .gallery {
    grid-template-columns: repeat(3, 1fr);
  }
```

```
}

/* When container >= 900px: 4 columns */
@container gallery (min-width: 900px) {
  .gallery {
    grid-template-columns: repeat(4, 1fr);
  }
}

.gallery img {
  width: 100%;
  height: auto;
  display: block;
  border-radius: var(--radius-md);
}
// src/components/PhotoGallery/PhotoGallery.tsx
import React from 'react';
import './PhotoGallery.css';

interface PhotoGalleryProps {
  images: string[];
}

export function PhotoGallery({ images }: PhotoGalleryProps) {
  return (
    <div className="gallery">
      {images.map((src, idx) => (
        <img key={idx} src={src} alt={`Gallery image ${idx +
1}`} />
      ))}
    </div>
  );
}
```

- **What it does:**
  - `.gallery` is marked as a container for inline-size queries.
  - Default grid: 2 columns; shifts to 3 or 4 when the component's width crosses 600px and 900px thresholds.
  - Images fill their grid cells, maintaining aspect ratio.
- **Why this approach:**
  - **Modularity:** Each `PhotoGallery` adapts to its own constraints.
  - **Simplicity:** No extra JavaScript; pure CSS handles layout.
  - **Reusability:** Use the same component in sidebars, modals, or full-page contexts.

Common Pitfalls

1. **Unsupported Browsers**
   - Container queries are new; some browsers may lack support.
   - **Fix:** Include a polyfill or feature detect and fall back to media queries.
2. **Forgetting `container-type`**
   - Without `container-type`, queries won't fire.
   - **Fix:** Always specify `container-type: inline-size;` on the element you query.
3. **Large DOM Trees**
   - Querying large containers can impact performance.
   - **Fix:** Scope container queries narrowly and avoid querying deep trees.

```
Gallery Container Queries

[Container Width < 600px]
┌──────────┐
│ [img][img] │  2 columns
└──────────┘

[600px ≤ Width < 900px]
┌───────────────┐
│[img][img][img]│ 3 columns
└───────────────┘

[Width ≥ 900px]
┌────────────────────┐
│[img][img][img][img]│ 4 columns
└────────────────────┘
```

Hands-On Exercise

Objective: Build a context-aware grid component using container queries.

1. **Component Setup:**
   - Scaffold `ResponsiveGrid.tsx` and `ResponsiveGrid.css`.
2. **Define Grid Defaults:**
   - In CSS, set `display: grid; gap: var(--spacing-3); grid-template-columns: repeat(1, 1fr);` and add `container-type: inline-size; container-name: grid`.
3. **Add Queries:**

    - `@container grid (min-width: 400px)` ⇒ 2 columns.
    - `@container grid (min-width: 800px)` ⇒ 3 columns.
    - `@container grid (min-width: 1200px)` ⇒ 4 columns.
4. **Test in Varying Contexts:**
    - Embed the grid in a narrow sidebar, main content area, and wide layout to observe column changes.
5. **Deliverable:**
    - `ResponsiveGrid` code and CSS.
    - Screenshots or a short GIF showing the grid reflow in different container widths.

Key Takeaways

- **Container Queries** let components adapt to their own size rather than the viewport.
- **CSS Grid** combined with `@container` empowers truly modular, context-aware layouts.
- Ensure browser support via polyfills and always declare `container-type` for query contexts.

Next Steps
Proceed to **Section 10.3**, where we'll explore **AI-Assisted Component Generation**—leveraging machine learning to accelerate component scaffolding and boilerplate creation.

10.3 AI-Assisted Component Generation

Goal Statement
In this section you'll learn how to leverage AI tools—such as GitHub Copilot, OpenAI Codex, or in-house ML models—to accelerate component scaffolding, boilerplate generation, and pattern synthesis, while maintaining code quality and consistency in your design system.

Key Terms

- **AI Pair Programming**
- **Prompt Engineering**
- **Template Generation**
- **Validation & Review**

- **Pattern Extraction**

Practical Outcome
By the end, you'll be equipped to integrate AI assistance into your workflow—crafting effective prompts, validating generated code, and iteratively refining AI outputs—to bootstrap new components, tests, and documentation in seconds without sacrificing maintainability.

Research & Gather Notes

- **Official Docs & Blogs**
  - GitHub Copilot documentation on "Autocompletion for React."
  - OpenAI Codex examples for "generate React components from prompts."
- **Community Examples**
  - Blog: "How Shopify uses AI to scaffold front-end patterns."
  - GitHub repo: community tools that generate Storybook stories via chat prompts.
- **Your Own Experience**
  - Noted that clear, structured prompts (including interface shape and styling tokens) yield highest-quality AI outputs.
  - Learned that always reviewing and linting AI-generated code prevents drift and errors.

AI-assisted tools can dramatically reduce the manual effort of writing repetitive code—boilerplate imports, prop type definitions, style hooks, and initial Storybook stories. By providing structured prompts describing the component's API, token usage, and desired behaviors, you can have the AI draft complete component files in seconds. However, to ensure consistency and correctness, you must review, test, and align these outputs with your design-system conventions.

A typical workflow:

1. **Define a Prompt Template:** Include component name, prop definitions, style tokens, and example usage.
2. **Invoke the AI Model:** Paste prompt into Copilot or call Codex programmatically.

3. **Review & Refine:** Manually audit generated JSX, CSS modules, and tests against lint rules.
4. **Iterate:** Provide feedback in the prompt or adjust the template to improve successive generations.

Concept Breakdown

1. **Prompt Engineering**
   - Crafting clear instructions and examples so the AI understands context, naming conventions, and style tokens.
2. **Component Templates**
   - Predefined prompt scaffolds that include import patterns, token references, and test stubs.
3. **Validation & Review**
   - Running linters, TypeScript type checks, unit tests, and visual snapshots on AI-generated code.
4. **Pattern Extraction**
   - Using AI to analyze existing components and infer best practices or common patterns for new scaffolding.
5. **Feedback Loop**
   - Iteratively improving prompts based on manual corrections to train the model in your project's idioms.

---

4. Code Walkthrough

Prompt Example:

```
Generate a React component named CardList that:
- lives in src/components/CardList/CardList.tsx
- accepts props: items: Array<{ id: string; title: string;
description: string }>
- uses CSS module 'CardList.module.css' with classNames:
container, card, title, description
- maps over items to render each card with title in h3 and
description in p
- includes a Storybook story file 'CardList.stories.tsx' with
Default and Empty states
- includes a test file 'CardList.test.tsx' using React
Testing Library
```

AI Output (excerpt):

```
// CardList.tsx
import React from 'react';
import styles from './CardList.module.css';

export interface CardListProps {
  items: { id: string; title: string; description: string
}[];
}

export const CardList: React.FC<CardListProps> = ({ items })
=> {
  if (!items.length) return <div
className={styles.container}>No items</div>;
  return (
    <div className={styles.container}>
      {items.map(item => (
        <div key={item.id} className={styles.card}>
          <h3 className={styles.title}>{item.title}</h3>
          <p
className={styles.description}>{item.description}</p>
        </div>
      ))}
    </div>
  );
};
```

- **What it does:** AI generated complete component, stories, and tests based on a structured prompt.
- **Why this approach:** Dramatically reduces manual boilerplate, letting you focus on refinement and edge cases.

Common Pitfalls

1. **Over-Reliance on AI**
   - Blindly accepting output may introduce subtle bugs or inconsistencies.
   - **Fix:** Always review, lint, and test generated code.
2. **Vague Prompts**
   - Broad or unclear instructions yield generic or incorrect code.
   - **Fix:** Include explicit requirements: prop types, style tokens, file paths, and examples.
3. **Token Misuse**
   - AI may hard-code values instead of using your design tokens.

   - **Fix:** Emphasize in the prompt: "use `tokens.spacing[2]`, `tokens.color.primary`," etc.

Hands-On Exercise

Objective: Use AI to scaffold a new component and refine it to your standards.

1. **Choose a Component:**
   - E.g., "NotificationBanner" accepting `message: string` and `type: 'success' | 'error'`.
2. **Craft a Prompt:**
   - Specify component name, props, CSS module file and class names, design tokens to use, and to generate stories/tests.
3. **Generate Code:**
   - Paste prompt into Copilot or Codex playground; let the AI produce files.
4. **Review & Lint:**
   - Run your linter, TypeScript compiler, and tests. Fix any errors or token misuse.
5. **Visual Verification:**
   - Add a Storybook story and confirm the component renders correctly with theme and tokens applied.
6. **Deliverable:**
   - A PR with `NotificationBanner.tsx`, `.module.css`, `.stories.tsx`, and `.test.tsx`—all AI-generated and manually validated.

Key Takeaways

- **AI-assisted generation** can accelerate boilerplate creation when guided by well-crafted prompts.
- **Review and validation** are essential to ensure consistency with your design-system conventions.
- **Iterative prompt refinement** and pattern extraction help AI produce higher-quality outputs over time.

Next Steps
Proceed to **Section 10.4**, where we'll explore **Evolving Standards: MDX, CSS Houdini, and Beyond**—emerging technologies that promise to further enhance component documentation, styling, and browser capabilities.

10.4 Evolving Standards: MDX, CSS Houdini, and Beyond

Goal Statement
In this section you'll learn how to adopt emerging web standards—**MDX** for rich component documentation, **CSS Houdini** for custom styling hooks, and other APIs (e.g., **CSS Container Queries Level 2**, **Web Components** interoperability)—to future-proof your React design system.

Key Terms

- **MDX**
- **CSS Houdini**
- **Paint & Layout Worklets**
- **Web Components**
- **Custom Properties API**

Practical Outcome
By the end, you'll know how to embed live React examples in Markdown via MDX, write a simple Houdini paint worklet to extend CSS, and understand the landscape of other standards that will shape component styling and interoperability going forward.

Research & Gather Notes

- **Official Specs & Guides**
  - MDX spec and Storybook's MDX integration.
  - W3C CSS Houdini Task Force drafts (Paint API, Typed OM).
- **Community Examples**
  - Storybook's docs using MDX for prop tables, examples, and note callouts.
  - CSS Houdini Paint Worklet demos (e.g. custom dotted borders).
- **Your Own Experience**

- Found MDX invaluable for combining narrative and live code.
- Early experiments with Houdini let us implement a "wavy underline" effect entirely in CSS.

As component libraries mature, documentation needs go beyond static code snippets. **MDX** bridges Markdown and JSX, letting you write prose, live examples, and property tables in one file. Meanwhile, **CSS Houdini** unlocks low-level access to the browser's styling engine via Paint and Layout Worklets, enabling bespoke visual effects—such as gradients that animate to data or fully custom grid algorithms—without heavy JS. Coupling these with Web Components support and evolving container/query standards ensures your design system remains cutting-edge and interoperable across frameworks.

Concept Breakdown

1. **MDX**
   - A markup format that mixes Markdown and React components, enabling fully interactive docs pages.
   - Used by Storybook Docs, Gatsby, Next.js.
2. **CSS Houdini**
   - A collection of low-level APIs (Paint, Layout, Typed OM) allowing JS to hook into CSS parsing and rendering.
   - Paint Worklets let you define `--custom-border: paint(wavyBorder)`.
3. **Web Components Interop**
   - Custom Elements, Shadow DOM, and HTML templates let your React components expose native-custom tags for consumption in non-React contexts.
4. **Emerging CSS Features**
   - **Container Queries Level 2** with size units and relational queries.
   - **Subgrid** support in Grid to let child grids inherit parent tracks.

Code Walkthroughs

A. MDX in Storybook

```
import { Meta, Story, ArgsTable } from '@storybook/addon-
docs';
import { Button } from './Button';

<Meta title="Atoms/Button" component={Button} />

# Button

Use the `<Button>` component for primary actions.

<Story name="Primary">
  <Button variant="primary">Primary Action</Button>
</Story>

<ArgsTable story="Primary" />
```

- Embeds live `<Button>` and auto-generated arg tables within Markdown narrative.

B. Simple Paint Worklet

```
// src/houdini/wavyBorder.js
class WavyBorderPainter {
  static get inputProperties() { return ['--wave-color', '--
wave-width']; }
  paint(ctx, geom) {
    const color = getComputedStyle(this).getPropertyValue('--
wave-color') || 'black';
    const width =
parseFloat(getComputedStyle(this).getPropertyValue('--wave-
width')) || 2;
    ctx.strokeStyle = color;
    ctx.lineWidth = width;
    ctx.beginPath();
    const { width: w, height: h } = geom;
    for (let x = 0; x <= w; x++) {
      const y = h/2 + Math.sin((x / w) * 4 * Math.PI) * 5;
      ctx.lineTo(x, y);
    }
    ctx.stroke();
  }
}
registerPaint('wavy-border', WavyBorderPainter);
/* Usage in your component's CSS */
.heading {
```

```
  --wave-color: #0077cc;
  --wave-width: 3;
  border-image: paint(wavy-border) 30 fill;
}
```

- Paint worklet draws a sine-wave border around elements.

```
MDX & Houdini Overview

[MDX File]
  Markdown text
  <ComponentExample />
  <ArgsTable />

[CSS Houdini]
  Paint Worklet → custom paint()
  CSS rule → paint(wavy-border)
```

Hands-On Exercise

Objective: Integrate MDX docs and a basic Houdini effect.

1. **MDX Documentation:**
   - Convert one of your component's docs from pure CSF to MDX, adding narrative, live example, and args table.
2. **Paint Worklet:**
   - Create a `highlightStripe` paint worklet that draws diagonal stripes.
   - Register it and apply via `background-image: paint(highlightStripe)` on a callout box in MDX.
3. **Verify:**
   - Run Storybook; confirm MDX docs render correctly and the CSS effect appears.

Key Takeaways

- **MDX** unifies docs and live examples, improving readability and exploration.
- **CSS Houdini** empowers novel styling patterns without heavy JS.
- Staying abreast of **Web Components**, **Container Queries**, and **Grid Subgrid** ensures your system remains future-ready.

Next Steps
Proceed to **Section 10.5**, where we'll delve into **Design System Governance in a Standardized Web Platform**—examining how W3C specs and industry groups shape shared component libraries across the web ecosystem.

`Emerging Technologies Comparison Table`

Technology	Description	Primary Use Case
MDX	Markdown + JSX for rich, interactive documentation	Embedding live component examples & props tables directly in docs
CSS Houdini (Paint API)	JS-driven paint worklets for custom styling	Creating bespoke visual effects (e.g., wavy borders, dynamic backgrounds)
CSS Container Queries	Query a component's container size, not the viewport	Adaptive component layouts based on their own width (e.g., responsive cards/grids)
Web Components	Framework-agnostic custom elements & Shadow DOM	Publishing React components as native HTML elements for cross-framework reuse
CSS Subgrid	Inherit parent grid tracks for nested grids	Building complex nested grid layouts with consistent alignment

10.5 End-of-Chapter Summary & Key Takeaways

1. **Server Components & Edge Rendering**
   - **Server Components** offload data fetching and initial rendering to the server/edge, sending minimal client bundles.
   - **Edge Rendering** via CDNs reduces latency, and the "islands" architecture hydrates only interactive parts on the client.
2. **Component-Level CSS Grid & Container Queries**
   - **CSS Grid** combined with `@container` queries lets components adapt their layout based on their own size, not just the viewport.

    - Declare `container-type: inline-size;` and use `@container` rules to shift grid templates dynamically.
3. **AI-Assisted Component Generation**
    - AI tools (Copilot, Codex) can scaffold components, stories, and tests from structured prompts, dramatically cutting boilerplate time.
    - Always **review, lint, and test** AI-generated code, and refine prompts to align with your design-token conventions.
4. **Evolving Web Standards**
    - **MDX** merges Markdown and JSX for richer, interactive documentation with live examples and prop tables.
    - **CSS Houdini** (Paint and Layout Worklets) empowers custom styling logic within the browser's rendering engine.
    - Keep an eye on **Web Components**, **CSS Subgrid**, and next-gen **Container Query** features to future-proof your library.

— These emerging patterns and technologies position your React design system for the next wave of performance, flexibility, and developer productivity—ensuring it remains robust and cutting-edge in the evolving web ecosystem.

10.6 Hands-On Exercises

Exercise 1: Implement a Server/Client Component Split

- **Objective:** Convert an existing component with data fetching into a Server Component and isolate its interactive parts as a Client Component.
- **Steps:**
    1. Identify a list or dashboard component that fetches data in your app.
    2. Rename it to `*.server.tsx`, move its data-fetching logic into the component body (so it runs on the server/edge).
    3. Extract any interactive UI (e.g. a "Refresh" button or filter controls) into a separate `*.client.tsx` file marked with `'use client'`.
    4. Render the server component and client island together in your page.
    5. Measure and compare bundle size and hydration time before and after.

- **Deliverable:** Code diff showing the split, and metrics illustrating reduced client payload.

Exercise 2: Build a Container-Query-Driven Grid

- **Objective:** Create a reusable `<ResponsiveGrid>` component that adapts its column count based on its own width.
- **Steps:**
  1. Scaffold `ResponsiveGrid.tsx` and `ResponsiveGrid.css`.
  2. In the CSS, declare `container-type: inline-size; container-name: grid;` on the root.
  3. Define default `grid-template-columns: repeat(1,1fr);` then use `@container grid (min-width: 400px)` for 2 columns, `(min-width: 800px)` for 3, `(min-width: 1200px)` for 4.
  4. In the component, render children inside a `<div className="grid">`.
  5. Test by embedding the grid in containers of varying widths (sidebar, main content).
- **Deliverable:** The component code plus screenshots or a short GIF demonstrating the grid's reflow.

Exercise 3: Scaffold a Component with AI and Refine It

- **Objective:** Use AI (Copilot or Codex) to generate a new component's boilerplate, then validate and polish the output.
- **Steps:**
  1. Choose a component to create (e.g. `AlertBanner` with `message`, `type` props).
  2. Write a prompt specifying file paths, prop types, CSS module, Storybook stories, and test stubs.
  3. Invoke the AI tool to generate the `.tsx`, `.module.css`, `.stories.tsx`, and `.test.tsx` files.
  4. Run your linter, TypeScript compiler, and tests; fix any issues or token misuses.
  5. Add a Storybook MDX doc showcasing the component with narrative and live examples.

- **Deliverable:** A PR containing the AI-generated files, with manual corrections, passing all checks.

Exercise 4: Create an MDX-Powered Documentation Page

- **Objective:** Convert one of your component's documentation to MDX, embedding live examples and props tables.
- **Steps:**
    1. Rename or create `ComponentName.stories.mdx`.
    2. Import `Meta`, `Story`, and `ArgsTable` from `@storybook/addon-docs`.
    3. Write Markdown headings and prose explaining the component's purpose.
    4. Embed `<Story name="Default" />` and `<ArgsTable of={Meta} />`.
    5. Run Storybook and verify the MDX page renders narrative, examples, and prop tables correctly.
- **Deliverable:** The `.mdx` file and a screenshot of the rendered Docs-Page.

Exercise 5: Experiment with a CSS Houdini Paint Worklet

- **Objective:** Write and register a simple Houdini paint worklet to apply a custom background effect.
- **Steps:**
    1. Create `stripePainter.js` defining `inputProperties` (e.g. `--stripe-color`) and a `paint(ctx, geom)` that draws diagonal stripes.
    2. Register the worklet via `CSS.paintWorklet.addModule()`.
    3. In a CSS file, apply `background-image: paint(stripePainter)` on a callout box, and set `--stripe-color`.
    4. Use that box in a React component and run in a browser that supports Houdini (or include a polyfill).
- **Deliverable:** The worklet code, CSS rules, and a screenshot showing the striped background effect.

These exercises will help you master the cutting-edge features of React design systems—server/edge rendering, container queries, AI-assisted scaffolding, MDX documentation, and Houdini styling—preparing your library for the web's future.

10.7 Next Steps: Experimenting with React Server Components

Goal Statement
In this section you'll learn how to set up a minimal React Server Components (RSC) experiment—so you can prototype, benchmark, and understand the developer ergonomics and performance characteristics of mixing server and client components in your own design-system context.

Key Terms

- **React Server Components (RSC)**
- **Next.js App Router**
- `use client` **Directive**
- **Streaming SSR**
- **Data Fetching on the Server**

Practical Outcome
By the end, you'll have a small Next.js "playground" app that uses RSC for data-heavy UI and client components for interactivity, and you'll be able to compare rendering times, bundle sizes, and hydration behavior against a fully client-side implementation.

Explanatory Text

While RSC are still evolving, a hands-on prototype is the best way to gauge their fit for your design system. You'll scaffold a Next.js project, create one list component as an RSC (fetching data server-side) and another as a client component (fetching in `useEffect`), then compare:

- **Bundle Size:** Does the RSC version exclude unnecessary JS?
- **Time to First Byte (TTFB):** How quickly does server-rendered content arrive?
- **Hydration Overhead:** How much JS is needed to hydrate interactive parts?

This experiment surfaces practical trade-offs—network cost vs. interactivity, streaming complexity, and tooling support—so you can decide where RSC make sense in your library.

Hands-On Exercise

Objective: Build and benchmark an RSC vs. client-side list.

1. **Scaffold Next.js App:**

```
npx create-next-app@latest rsc-playground --experimental-app
cd rsc-playground
```

2. **Implement Server Component:**
   - Create `app/users/UserList.server.tsx`:

```
import React from 'react';
export default async function UserList() {
  const res = await
fetch('https://jsonplaceholder.typicode.com/users');
  const users = await res.json();
  return (
    <ul>
      {users.map(u => <li key={u.id}>{u.name}</li>)}
    </ul>
  );
}
```

   - Import it on the home page alongside a client version.
3. **Implement Client Component:**
   - Create `components/UserList.client.tsx` using `useEffect/useState` to fetch and render the same list.
4. **Measure Metrics:**

    - **Bundle Size:** Run `next build && next export` and inspect `.next/static` sizes.
    - **TTFB:** Use `curl -w "%{time_starttransfer}\n"` against your deployed preview.
    - **Hydration JS:** In browser devtools, note JS loaded to hydrate the page.
5. **Analyze & Document:**
    - Compare the server vs. client versions in a markdown file:
        - Bundle size differences
        - TTFB numbers
        - Hydration payloads
    - Note observations: where RSC shines and where it introduces complexity.

End-of-Section Summary

- A small RSC prototype clarifies real-world benefits: reduced client bundles and faster initial loads.
- Measuring TTFB and hydration costs reveals trade-offs between server rendering and client interactivity.
- This experiment informs where—and for which components—React Server Components can best serve your design system's performance and maintainability goals.

Appendices

A. Glossary of Terms and Acronyms

- **Accessibility (a11y)**
  Ensuring that UI components are usable by people with disabilities, often via ARIA roles, keyboard navigation, and proper semantics.
- **Args**
  In Storybook, a mechanism for defining component inputs (props) that can be edited interactively via the Controls panel.
- **Atomic Component**
  The smallest, indivisible UI element in a design system (e.g., Button, Input).
- **Bundle Size**
  The total size of JavaScript and assets shipped to the client for an application or component library.
- **CI/CD**
  Continuous Integration / Continuous Deployment: automated pipelines that build, test, and deploy code changes.
- **Component-Driven Development (CDD)**
  A workflow that emphasizes building and testing UI components in isolation before integrating them into an application.
- **Container Query**
  A CSS feature (`@container`) that applies styles to an element based on the size of its container rather than the viewport.
- **Context API**
  React feature for passing values (state, callbacks) deeply through the component tree without prop drilling.
- **CSR**
  Client-Side Rendering: rendering the UI in the browser after downloading JavaScript.
- **CSS Houdini**
  A set of low-level browser APIs (Paint, Layout, Typed OM) that allow developers to extend CSS with custom worklets.
- **CSS-in-JS**
  A styling approach where CSS is written and scoped within JavaScript files, often leveraging libraries like styled-components or Emotion.
- **HTML Custom Element (Web Component)**
  A framework-agnostic custom HTML tag defined via the Web Components standards (Custom Elements, Shadow DOM).

- **HOC (Higher-Order Component)**
  A React pattern where a function takes a component and returns an enhanced component with additional props or behavior.
- **Islands Architecture**
  A rendering approach where static parts of the page are server-rendered as HTML, and only small "islands" of interactivity are hydrated on the client.
- **JSX**
  JavaScript syntax extension that looks like HTML, used to define React component trees.
- **MDX**
  A markup format combining Markdown and JSX, used for writing interactive documentation in Storybook or static sites.
- **Monorepo**
  A single repository that houses multiple related projects or packages, often managed via Lerna or Nx.
- **RICE Scoring**
  A prioritization framework using Reach, Impact, Confidence, and Effort to calculate task priority:
  RICEScore=(Reach × Impact × Confidence) / EffortRICE Score = (Reach × Impact × Confidence) / Effort.
- **React.memo**
  A React API that memoizes a component, preventing re-renders when its props haven't changed (shallow comparison).
- **Render Props**
  A pattern where a component's child is a function that receives state or callbacks and returns JSX, enabling flexible composition.
- **RSC (React Server Component)**
  A React component that runs on the server or edge, fetches data, and streams HTML to the client without shipping its code to the browser.
- **Semantic Versioning (SemVer)**
  A versioning scheme (`MAJOR.MINOR.PATCH`) that communicates the nature of changes:
    - **PATCH**: bug fixes
    - **MINOR**: backward-compatible features
    - **MAJOR**: breaking changes
- **Server-Side Rendering (SSR)**
  Rendering HTML on the server before sending it to the client, improving initial load performance and SEO.
- **Scoped CSS Variable**
  A CSS custom property (e.g., `--color-primary`) defined at a specific scope (e.g., `:root` or `.theme-dark`) for theming.

- **Strangler Pattern**
  An incremental migration strategy that "strangles" legacy code by gradually replacing it with new implementations via routing or aliasing.
- **Subgrid**
  A CSS Grid feature that allows nested grids to inherit track definitions from their parent grid.
- **Storybook**
  An open-source tool for developing, testing, and documenting UI components in isolation.
- **Technical Debt**
  The implied cost of additional rework caused by choosing an easy solution now instead of a better approach that would take longer.
- **Token (Design Token)**
  A named value representing a design decision (e.g., color, spacing, typography) that can be referenced consistently across code and design.
- **Typed OM (Typed Object Model)**
  A CSS Houdini API that exposes CSS values (lengths, colors) as typed JavaScript objects rather than raw strings.
- **Visual Regression Testing**
  Automated comparison of UI snapshots (e.g., via Chromatic or Percy) to detect unintended visual changes.
- **Web Components**
  A set of standardized browser APIs (Custom Elements, Shadow DOM, HTML templates) for creating reusable, encapsulated HTML tags.
- **Workspaces**
  A package manager feature (Yarn or npm) that allows multiple packages in a single repository to share dependencies and link locally.

Appendix B: Storybook Configuration Cheat Sheet

File / Command	Purpose & Key Snippets
Install Storybook	`bash npx sb init --builder webpack5 `
.storybook/main.js	**```jsmodule.exports = { stories: ['../src/components/**/*.stories.@(js**
.storybook/preview.js	`js import React from 'react'; import { ThemeProvider } from`

File / Command	Purpose & Key Snippets

	'../src/theme/ThemeProvider';
	import '../src/styles/index.css';
	
	export const decorators = [
	 (Story) => (
	 <ThemeProvider>
	 <Story />
	 </ThemeProvider>
	),
	];
	
	export const parameters = {
	 actions: { argTypesRegex: '^on[A-Z].*' },
	 controls: { expanded: true },
	 a11y: { element: '#root' },
	};

Story Scripts	jsonc
	// package.json
	{
	 "scripts": {
	 "storybook": "start-storybook -p 6006",
	 "build-storybook": "build-storybook --output-dir storybook-static"
	 }
	}

Essential Addons	- @storybook/addon-essentials **(Actions, Controls, Docs)-** @storybook/addon-a11y **(Accessibility)-** @storybook/addon-interactions **(Playwright integration)**

Custom Webpack Aliases	**Mirror app aliases for consistency:**js
	config.resolve.alias = {
	 '@components': path.resolve(__dirname, '../src/components'),
	 '@styles': path.resolve(__dirname, '../src/styles'),
	};

MDX Docs Setup	mdx import { Meta, Story, ArgsTable } from '@storybook/addon-docs'; import { Button } from './Button'; <Meta title="Atoms/Button" component={Button} /> # Button <Story name="Primary"><Button>Click</Button></Story> <ArgsTable story="Primary" />
Visual Regression (Chromatic)	**1. Install:** npm install --save-dev chromatic**2. Script:** "chromatic": "chromatic --project-token $CHROMATIC_TOKEN --exit-zero-on-changes"**3. CI step:** npm run chromatic
Common Pitfalls	**- Missing** preview.js **imports → unstyled stories- Glob mismatch in** main.js **→ stories not detected- Alias mismatch → import errors- Over-nesting decorators → slow story render**

Use this cheat sheet to quickly verify and set up your Storybook configuration, ensuring consistency with your React design system's patterns and workflows.

Appendix C: TypeScript Utility Types for Design Tokens

Below are common utility types and patterns to type your design tokens safely and ergonomically.

```
// 1. DeepPartial: make all nested properties optional
export type DeepPartial<T> = {
  [P in keyof T]?: T[P] extends object ? DeepPartial<T[P]> :
T[P];
};

// 2. TokenMap: enforce that a token set matches a key/value
shape
export type TokenMap<Keys extends string | number | symbol,
Value> = {
  [K in Keys]: Value;
};

// Example: a color token set where each key maps to a CSS
color string
export type ColorTokens = TokenMap<'primary' | 'secondary' |
'background' | 'text', string>;

// 3. TokenScale: numeric scales (e.g. spacing or typography)
export type TokenScale<Size extends string | number = string,
T = number> = Record<Size, T>;

// Example: spacing scale from 0 to 5
export interface SpacingTokens {
  0: 0;
  1: 4;
  2: 8;
  3: 16;
  4: 24;
  5: 32;
}

// 4. MergeTokens: merge default tokens with user overrides
safely
export type MergeTokens<Defaults, Overrides extends
Partial<Defaults>> =
  Omit<Defaults, keyof Overrides> & Overrides;
```

```
// 5. TokenKeyOf: helper to extract valid token keys
export type TokenKeyOf<T> = keyof T;

// Example: 'primary' | 'secondary' | 'background' | 'text'
type ColorKey = TokenKeyOf<ColorTokens>;

// 6. ResponsiveTokens: mapping breakpoints to token values
export type ResponsiveTokens<Token> = Record<'sm' | 'md' |
'lg' | 'xl', Token>;

// Example: responsive font size
export type FontSizeTokens = ResponsiveTokens<string>;

// 7. Typed CSS Variables: generate CSS custom-property
strings from tokens
export type CSSVar<T extends string> = `var(--${T})`;

// Usage: CSSVar<'color-primary'> yields 'var(--color-
primary)'

// 8. ExtractTokenPaths: flatten nested token object into
dot-notation keys
export type DotPath<T, Prev extends string = ''> = {
  [K in keyof T & string]: T[K] extends object
    ? DotPath<T[K], `${Prev}${K}.`>
    : `${Prev}${K}`;
}[keyof T & string];

// Given
interface ThemeTokens {
  color: {
    primary: string;
    secondary: string;
  };
  spacing: {
    small: number;
    large: number;
  };
}
// DotPath<ThemeTokens> => 'color.primary' |
'color.secondary' | 'spacing.small' | 'spacing.large'

// 9. ThemeTokens interface example
export interface ThemeTokens {
  color: Record<'primary' | 'secondary' | 'background' |
'text', string>;
  spacing: Record<'xs' | 'sm' | 'md' | 'lg' | 'xl', number>;
  typography: {
    fontSize: Record<'sm' | 'md' | 'lg', string>;
    fontWeight: Record<'normal' | 'bold', number>;
  };
```

```
}

// 10. Use DeepPartial for overrides
export type ThemeOverride = DeepPartial<ThemeTokens>;

// 11. Utility to derive CSS variables object from tokens:
export function toCSSVars<T extends Record<string,
any>>(tokens: T, prefix = ''): Record<string, string> {
  const vars: Record<string, string> = {};
  Object.entries(tokens).forEach(([key, value]) => {
    const varName = `--${prefix}${key}`;
    if (typeof value === 'object') {
      Object.assign(vars, toCSSVars(value, `${prefix}${key}-
`));
    } else {
      vars[varName] = String(value);
    }
  });
  return vars;
}
```

These utility types help you:

- **Enforce token shapes** (`TokenMap`, `TokenScale`)
- **Allow safe overrides** (`DeepPartial`, `MergeTokens`)
- **Extract valid keys** (`TokenKeyOf`, `DotPath`)
- **Integrate with CSS** (`CSSVar`, `toCSSVars`)

Use these patterns to maintain strict type safety and consistency across your design-system tokens.

Appendix D: Helpful Tools and Resources

- **Design & Prototyping**
  - **Figma** – Collaborative UI design with Team Libraries and plug-ins like Figma Tokens.
  - **FigJam** – For whiteboarding, planning roadmaps, and RFC brainstorming.
- **Component Development & Documentation**
  - **Storybook** – Isolated component dev environment with Controls, Docs, and A11y addons.
  - **MDX** – Embeds live React components in Markdown for rich documentation.
  - **Style Dictionary** – Automates token export from JSON to platform-specific styles.

- **Testing & Quality**
    - **Chromatic** – Visual regression testing built on top of Storybook.
    - **@axe-core/react** – Accessibility linting and runtime checks.
    - **Jest & React Testing Library** – Unit and integration tests for React components.
- **Build & Release**
    - **semantic-release** – Fully automated semantic versioning and changelog generation.
    - **Lerna / Nx** – Monorepo management with workspaces, bootstrapping, and task orchestration.
    - **GitHub Actions** – CI/CD workflows for lint, test, build, and release pipelines.
- **Performance & Analysis**
    - **webpack-bundle-analyzer / source-map-explorer** – Visualize and audit bundle composition.
    - **React DevTools Profiler** – Measure component render timings and identify performance bottlenecks.
    - **Lighthouse CLI** – Automated page-load and runtime performance audits.
- **Styling & Layout**
    - **CSS Houdini** – Paint/Layout Worklets for custom CSS effects.
    - **PostCSS** – Plugin-based CSS processing (autoprefixer, nesting).
    - **Tailwind CSS** – Utility-first framework for rapid styling.
- **AI & Automation**
    - **GitHub Copilot / OpenAI Codex** – AI-assisted code generation and boilerplate scaffolding.
    - **Plop.js** – Micro-generator framework for custom file scaffolding scripts.
- **Community & Learning**
    - **Design Systems Slack** – Community channel for DS practitioners.
    - **React Summit / JSNation** – Conferences featuring design-system talks.
    - **"Keep a Changelog"** – Guide for consistent changelog formatting and maintenance.

Keep this appendix as your go-to reference when choosing the right tools for each phase of your design-system journey.

Index

Printed in Poland
by Amazon Fulfillment
Poland Sp. z o.o., Wrocław

60312441R00142